IOO
perfect pairings

main dishes to enjoy with wines you love

JILL SILVERMAN HOUGH

PHOTOGRAPHS BY LUCY SCHAEFFER

WILEY

JOHN WILEY & SONS, INC.

Published by John Wiley & Sons, Inc., Hoboken, New Jersey
Published simultaneously in Canada

Library of Congress Cataloging-in-Publication Data

Hough, Jill Silverman.
  100 perfect pairings : main dishes to enjoy with wines you love / Jill Silverman
Hough.
     p. cm.
  Includes index.
  ISBN 978-0-470-44634-8 (cloth)
  1. Cookery. 2. Wine and wine making. I. Title.
  TX7714.H692 2011
  641.5--dc22
                                   2010010790

Printed in China

10 9 8 7 6 5 4 3 2 1

To my awesome,
incredible,
amazing,
perfect dad,
who I love more than
words can say

acknowledgments

Judy Washington, I'm so very, very lucky to be the recipient of your incredible generosity. Thank you for your time, your taste buds, and your friendship. I'm better for all three.

To my fabulous recipe testers—Lori Adleman, Kate and Allan Aks, Kay Austin, Melissa Austin, John Danby, Pam Crowley Fischer, Lynn Forsey, Randy Guerrero, Michael and Lanniece Hall, Janie Duthie Humphrey, Rhodora Javier, Jan Kroeger, the McIver family, Meredith Medin, Rachel Meserve, Deirdre Spero Nair, Susan and David Norman, Susan Pruett, Keven Seaver, Andrea Stupka, and Suzanne S. Young—whether your specific feedback is included in these pages or not, know that you contributed to this book, and me, a thousand-fold. Thank you for ridiculously spending your spare time helping me to do my work. You are angels.

To my amazing agent, Jennifer Griffin, and everyone at the Miller Agency—I'm honored to work with you. Truly.

To Linda Ingroia, Liz Britten, and everyone at Wiley—thank you for your patience, your wisdom, and your expertise. Thanks, too, to the Wiley publicity department, for taking such good care of me.

To Lucy Schaeffer, Simon Andrews, Penelope Bouklas, and their talented assistants—could my recipes be any more beautiful? I think not, and I thank you.

Elizabeth Van Itallie, I love your gorgeous book design.

And to Mia Malm and Constellation Wines—many thanks once again for your wine donation.

Finally, thank you to my family for giving me the gift of good food. Thank you to my husband for being there for every bite and sip. And I've said it before, but there's no saying it that's enough—thank you to my friends and family for your love and support, in this and all things. Thank you all, mostly, for the wonderful life I lead. I love you.

contents

about this book

Here's the thing that most food and wine books don't tell you: You don't have to be a food and wine pairing expert to thoroughly appreciate and enjoy good combinations of food and wine.

It's kind of like saying that you don't have to be a mechanic to enjoy driving a car—pretty obvious, right?—and yet most food and wine books would have you believe that you have to first *learn* food and wine pairing before you can *do* food and wine pairing and then *enjoy* great combinations of food and wine.

I say they've got it all wrong. You don't have to know all the dishes that pair well with, say, Cabernet Sauvignon, or why they do, to make one of them and say, "Damn, that's good!" as you enjoy it with a glass of Cabernet.

So with this book, you get to cut to the chase. Like my original *100 Perfect Pairings* book featuring small plates recipes, all you have to do is open to the Cabernet chapter, pick a recipe, make it, and pour yourself a glass of Cab as you sit down to eat.

It's that simple.

Also like my original book, this one covers twelve of the most basic wine varieties, wines you can find almost anywhere you shop. There might be a variety or two that are new to you, but they're good food wines worth knowing.

And every recipe in each chapter will go with every bottle of that wine variety. Some recipes might work better with certain styles of, for example, Sauvignon Blanc, but they'll all work with Sauvignon Blanc. If you know that your particular bottle of Sauvignon Blanc is grassy or that it's citrusy, great. If not, don't worry about it.

At all.

VARIETAL NAMES: WE SAY PINOT NOIR, THEY SAY BURGUNDY

In the United States, we label our wines varietally, or by the type of grape that was used to make the wine, like Chardonnay or Pinot Noir. And so the recipes in this book are divided by those varietal names. In other parts of the world, though, wine might be labeled by where it's from. French Burgundy, for example. To know what wine variety that might be like, you'd have to know that in Burgundy, they grow mostly Chardonnay and Pinot Noir grapes. So red Burgundy is essentially what we'd call Pinot Noir.

But you don't need to remember that. At the beginning of each chapter is a list of other names the wine can go by.

---

so what exactly *is* a perfect pairing?

Some say a good food and wine pairing is one where neither element overwhelms the other, where they're complementary.

Some say a good food and wine pairing is one where the food
doesn't change the taste of the wine, or if it does, it changes for the
better. To test this, you take a sip of wine, you take a bite of food,
and then you take a sip of wine again—and the second sip doesn't
taste different from the first. Or if the wine does taste different, it
tastes better—the bitterness was softened, for example.

I say it doesn't have to be that scientific. All you have to do is try
a food and a wine together and you either like the combination or
you don't.

A perfect pairing is your call.

does every pair have to be perfect?

I recently went to a fantastic dinner party. The table groaned with
delicious things to eat and drink. Did they all go together perfectly?
Not at all. Did we care? Not at all. We were too busy talking, laugh-
ing, eating, drinking, and enjoying our hosts' hospitality.

Really, there are a lot more important things to pay attention to—
at the table and in life. If food and wine pairing is something you're
interested in, play and explore. But definitely—definitely!—don't
worry about being perfect all the time.

how to use this book

To experience great combinations of food and wine, just open the
chapter for the wine you want to serve, make any recipe, then sit
down and enjoy the two together. That's all you have to do.

Should you want to learn a little more about food and wine pairing, check out the next section, A Really Brief Discussion of Food
and Wine Pairing (page 8). And look at the information at the beginning of each chapter, which will include the wine variety's broad
characteristics and tips for pairing recipes with it. Additional tips and
info are sprinkled throughout the book—pay attention to them only
to the degree that you're interested in knowing more.

the recipes

The entrée recipes in this book are what I like to call simple yet
special—dishes that don't take a lot of doing, but that nevertheless
make you and your tablemates feel indulged.

Some recipes are more quick and easy than others, and some might take several hours from beginning to end. But none requires lots of hard work, skill, or knowledge. Still, read each recipe once or twice before you start cooking, to avoid last-minute surprises.

If you like to riff and make a recipe your own, feel free. Just know that changing the recipe could change the perfection of the pairing.

the ingredients

It takes just as much time and effort to make a tomato salad with a good tomato as with a great one, but if you start with a great one, your finished dish will be that much more delicious. For that reason, I recommend using the best, most in-season ingredients you can find and that your budget will allow.

And for reasons of both flavor and ecological consciousness, consider buying from local, sustainable sources. For sustainable seafood options, check out www.seafoodwatch.org or the Marine Stewardship Council at www.msc.org.

the salt

Saltiness is key to food and wine pairing. So it's ideal if you use the same kind of coarse kosher salt that I used to develop these recipes—Diamond Crystal kosher salt. It's inexpensive and readily available. If you prefer to use table salt, or any other finely ground salt, note that it has about twice the saltiness, by volume, as Diamond Crystal. So use about half as much. The same goes for Morton's kosher salt.

And speaking of salt, in addition to using unsalted butter, as most recipes do these days, these recipes use reduced-sodium broths. Since saltiness can vary widely from brand to brand, using salt-free or low-salt ingredients puts you more in control of the outcome.

MAGIC IN YOUR MOUTH?

One of the reasons that certain combinations of food and wine really work, and others don't, is that food quite literally has the ability to alter how wine tastes. With one food, a wine might taste great. With another, not so much.

This wine-changing phenomenon is one of the things that can make food and wine pairing intimidating. And yet we all know that if you combine sugar and lemon juice, the sugar will make the lemon juice taste less sour. In other words, we know that foods can affect each other, but if we haven't had a lot of practice with food and wine, in that arena those same effects can seem mysterious.

They are pretty amazing—but also very learnable.

---

a really brief discussion of food and wine pairing

(Warning: It's not important to understand any of this to enjoy the recipes in this book.) We've all heard a lot about how this wine tastes jammy and that one is aromatic, and those nuances can come into play. But in pairing a food with a wine, or vice versa, the most important factors are the wine's broader characteristics, not the nuances. And those broad characteristics are:

- the wine's sweetness or dryness (lack of sweetness)
- the wine's acidity, crispness, or brightness
- the wine's tannins (which cause that bitter, dry-mouth feeling you often get from a red wine)
- the wine's weight or richness (how light or heavy it feels in your mouth)
- the wine's intensity (how subtle or strong its flavors are)

To create great food and wine combinations, the trick is to be familiar with these characteristics for each wine variety—or at least the ones you like—and then apply a few general tips about what works and what doesn't.

general pairing tips

■ 1. Pair sweet foods with sweet wines. *For example, chocolate and Port.* If you pair a sweet food with an unsweet, or dry, wine, it can make the wine taste sour or, in a red wine, it can accentuate those bitter, dry-mouth tannins. Even a dish that's just a little sweet, like honey-glazed ham, can have enough sweetness to make a dry wine taste less than ideal. So while sweet dishes need sweet wines, slightly sweet dishes often need slightly sweet, or off-dry, wines.

■ 2. Pair acidic foods with acidic wines. *For example, salad with a vinai-grette dressing and Sauvignon Blanc.* If you pair a not-very-acidic food with an acidic wine, it can make the wine taste more acidic, and sometimes downright sour.

■ 3. Pair rich/meaty/heavy, acidic, or slightly bitter foods with tannic wines (wines that give you that bitter, dry-mouth feeling you often get from a red wine). *For example, charbroiled steak with mustard sauce and Cabernet Sauvignon.* If you choose a food that fails to somehow account for the tannins in a wine, it can make the wine taste even more tannic, and sometimes unpalatably bitter.

4. Pair light foods with light wines and heavy foods with heavy wines. *For example, tomato salad and Pinot Grigio, or Brie baked in puff pastry and Chardonnay.* If you pair a light food with a heavy wine, or vice versa, things won't necessarily taste bad, they'll just seem out of balance.

5. Pair intense foods with intense wines. *For example, peppercorn steak and Syrah.* As with the preceding tip, this helps prevent one component from overwhelming the other.

6. When considering a dish, consider its most expressive components. In other words, when deciding if your dish is sweet, acidic, rich/meaty/heavy, bitter, light, or intensely flavored, or some combination, don't look to its main ingredient. Consider the dish as a whole, identify the dominant flavors and textures, and then let *those* elements inform your wine choice.

For example, fillet of sole with cream sauce and Chardonnay. In this example, the light fish might suggest a light wine. But the most expressive component of the dish isn't the fish—it's the cream sauce. And since that's rich, according to General Pairing Tip 4, the dish would be best with a rich wine.

fine-tuning tips

Once the basic principles are in play, you can do some fine-tuning. You'll notice that many of the recipes in this book suggest that you taste the final dish with your wine and adjust. That can really make the difference between a good combination and a perfect pairing.

1. More salt or acid in the food will decrease the experience of acid and tannin, or that dry-mouth bitterness, and increase the experience of fruit or sweetness in the wine. *For example, if your food is making your wine taste sour, add salt or something acidic, like lemon or lime juice, vinegar, or buttermilk, to the recipe.* This is the adjustment that gets used most often because, in general, all wines are pretty acidic and red wines are pretty tannic. At the least, you want your food to hold up to those characteristics and, at the most, you want it to soften them.

2. More sweet or savory elements in the food will increase the experience of acid and tannin, or bitterness, and decrease the experience of fruit or sweetness in a wine. *For example, if your food is making your wine taste too sweet or like it has lost its crispness, add something sweet, like fruit or honey, or something savory, like cured meats, aged cheese, or* *mushrooms, to the recipe.* More often than not, though, the problem will be too much sweetness or savory-ness in your food, increasing the experience of acid and tannins and decreasing the experience of fruit and sweetness in your wine. To fix this, add salt or acid to the food, per Fine-Tuning Tip 1, or switch to a sweeter wine, per General Pairing Tip 1.

▥ 3. More rich or creamy elements in the food will help it pair with a rich or heavy wine. *For example, if your food is too light for your wine, add something rich or creamy, like butter, mayonnaise, avocado, or cream.*

▥ 4. Wine *in* the food almost always helps wine *go* with the food. *For example, if you want to help a sauce, soup, or stew work with a wine, add some of that wine to the sauce, soup, or stew.* A small splash will help a little. A big pour will sometimes help a lot.

nuances

If all you paid attention to were a wine's broad characteristics—sweetness, acidity, tannins, weight, and intensity—you'd have a near-perfect pairing every time.

But beyond those major influences, there are nuances. Here's where the jammy flavors and the aromatic qualities come into play. Some nuances tend to be characteristic of the wine variety, so there's information about typical nuances at the beginning of each chapter.

Some nuances, however, tend to be characteristic of particular producers, regions, or vintages (years). If you know those particulars, you can work with them. If you don't, don't worry about it.

sauvignon blanc

If you like sour candies, lemon meringue pie, or bright vinaigrette dressing, you probably like Sauvignon Blanc. Like those foods, Sauvignon Blanc has a good amount of tart acidity, a quality that can make it refreshing, but also sometimes downright mouth-puckering.

You can avoid that pucker if you account for Sauvignon Blanc's acidity in the foods you pair with it. Dishes with similarly bright notes are your best bet—they'll match up to zingy Sauvignon Blanc, softening it and making it a crisp, refreshing indulgence.

sauvignon blanc by another name

• **Bordeaux, White Bordeaux.** As with other French wines, these French Sauvignon Blancs are labeled with the name of the area they're from. They might have the general area name Bordeaux, or names of subregions within Bordeaux (Graves, for example). Basically, any white wine from Bordeaux will be made from Sauvignon Blanc grapes, typically blended with some Sémillion. • **Sancerre, Pouilly-Fumé.** These names come from areas in France's Loire Valley known for Sauvignon Blanc. • **Fumé Blanc.** Robert Mondavi is credited with coining this term, combining Sauvignon Blanc with Pouilly-Fumé. His winery still uses the name, and others have adopted it, too. Fumé Blancs often have some oak aging—that is, they're aged in contact with some form of oak—which can impart a lightly smoky quality.

pairing with sauvignon blanc

Although there are, of course, nuances to Sauvignon Blanc, the most important factors in food and wine pairing aren't a wine's nuances, but its broad strokes. If you learn a wine's overall characteristics and combine that information with the General Pairing Tips (page 8), you'll have a near-perfect pairing every time.

Broad characteristics:
- dry (not sweet)
- high in acidity, crispness, or brightness
- no or very low tannins
- light to medium weight
- medium intensity

Pairs well with dishes that are:

- not sweet
- high in acidity, crispness, or brightness
- light to medium weight
- medium intensity

(Because the wine has no or very low tannins, they're not a factor.)
For example, salad with vinaigrette dressing, sole with lemon-caper sauce, or vegetable soup with a splash of buttermilk.

fine-tuning

Because the most dominant characteristic of Sauvignon Blanc is the acid, when pairing with this wine, adding salt and/or acid to your food will almost always help. (For more about salt and acid in food effecting acidity in wine, see Fine-Tuning Tip 1 on page 9.)

To mimic the light, white qualities in the wine, lighter, whiter acids tend to work best—lemon juice, white wine or champagne vinegar, white or golden balsamic vinegar, buttermilk, and even sour cream. Very mild and refreshing spiciness can also add brightness, like the light tickle of watercress or a dab of horseradish.

Completely, and admittedly maddeningly, contrary to General Pairing Tip 4 (page 9), you can also sometimes use Sauvignon Blanc's high acidity to cut through bright but richer foods.

other nuances

Once you have a pairing that's working on the basis of sweetness, acidity, weight, and intensity, you can start playing with subtler nuances.

Some of the subtle flavors that you might find in a Sauvignon Blanc include grassiness, herbs, citrus (especially grapefruit), green apple, asparagus, bell pepper, a touch of smokiness (especially with Pouilly-Fumé and Fumé Blanc), and minerality. So it works to add those flavors, or foods that complement them, to your dishes.

other thoughts

Some foods that are considered classic pairings with Sauvignon Blanc are goat cheeses, fish and shellfish, chicken, salad with vinaigrette dressing, asparagus, tomatoes, and green vegetables.

asparagus soufflé

The beautiful thing about a soufflé is that although it seems special occasion and fancy, a soufflé is really quite simple to make, requiring no great culinary skill. Serve this spring-inspired version with a crisp green salad and a hunk of good bread and you've got the makings of an easy yet elegant brunch, lunch, or dinner. ▪ **Serves 4 to 6**

    1 **pound asparagus** (about 1 standard-sized bunch), trimmed and cut into rough 1-inch pieces (you should have 2¾ to 3 cups)
    3 **tablespoons unsalted butter,** plus more for buttering the soufflé mold(s)
    ¼ **cup all-purpose flour**
    1 **cup buttermilk** (reduced-fat is okay)
    5 **large egg yolks**
       Finely grated zest of 2 lemons (about 2 teaspoons packed)
    2 **teaspoons coarse kosher salt**
    1 **teaspoon white pepper,** ideally freshly ground
    7 **large egg whites**
       Special equipment: one 6-cup, four 1½-cup, or six 1-cup soufflé molds or ramekins

▨ Preheat the oven to 375°F. Butter one 6-cup soufflé mold, four 1½-cup soufflé molds, or six 1-cup soufflé molds. If using 4 or 6 molds, arrange them on a rimmed baking sheet. Set aside.

▨ In a large saucepan of boiling, well-salted water (1 tablespoon of coarse kosher salt per quart), cook the asparagus until very tender, 3 to 4 minutes. Drain and transfer to a blender or food processor and process to puree, scraping down the bowl as necessary. Set aside.

▨ If necessary, wipe out the saucepan and return it to the stovetop over medium heat. Add the butter. Once it's melted, add the flour and cook, whisking, for 1 minute. Add the buttermilk and cook, whisking, for 1 minute. Remove the pan from the heat and stir in the asparagus, egg yolks, lemon zest, salt, and pepper. Set aside.

▨ Use an electric mixer to whip the egg whites to soft peaks. Fold the egg whites into the asparagus mixture. Spoon the mixture into the prepared mold(s). (If making 4 or 6 smaller soufflés, you can prepare them up to 4 hours in advance, storing them covered in the refrigerator.)

▨ Bake until the soufflé is nicely browned and firm on top, but still slightly wobbly when you remove it from the oven, 30 to 35 minutes for 1 soufflé or about 20 minutes for 4 or 6. (If you prepared the soufflés in advance, they can go right from the refrigerator to the oven, but add 5 to 7 minutes of cooking time.) Serve hot.

risotto primavera

I love risotto for food and wine pairing because it's so malleable. Add vernal vegetables, goat cheese, and white wine, and it works with Sauvignon Blanc. Add steak, Parmesan, and red wine, and it works with Cabernet. And, with near-endless combinations of add-ins, cheese, and wine, you can make it work with pretty much anything in between. **Serves 6**

         6 cups reduced-sodium chicken or vegetable broth
        ¼ cup extra virgin olive oil
         1 onion, cut into ¼-inch dice
         1 large carrot, cut into ¼-inch dice
      1½ teaspoons coarse kosher salt, or more to taste
        ½ teaspoon freshly ground black pepper, or more to taste
      1½ cups Arborio rice
        ½ cup Sauvignon Blanc, or other dry white wine
        ½ pound asparagus (about half of a standard-sized bunch), trimmed and
            diagonally cut into ½-inch pieces (you should have about 1½ cups)
        ½ cup fresh or frozen peas, thawed if frozen
         6 scallions, white and light green parts only, diagonally cut into ¼-inch pieces
         2 tablespoons coarsely chopped fresh flat-leaf parsley
         1 tablespoon coarsely chopped fresh tarragon
        ¾ cup chèvre (spreadable goat cheese) (about 4 ounces), divided

▥ In a medium saucepan over high heat, bring the broth to a boil. Reduce the heat to very low, to keep the broth just below a simmer.

▥ In a large saucepan or small stockpot over medium heat, warm the olive oil. Add the onion and cook, stirring occasionally, until very soft, 6 to 8 minutes (adjust the heat, if necessary, to avoid browning). Add the carrot, salt, and pepper and cook, stirring occasionally, until the carrot is crisp-tender, about 2 minutes. Stir in the rice. Add the wine and cook, stirring, until the wine is absorbed. Ladle in about 1½ cups of broth. Stir constantly until almost all of the broth is absorbed, adjusting the heat to maintain a simmer. Continue adding broth, about ½ cup at a time, and stirring almost constantly, adding more broth when almost all of the previous addition is absorbed.

▥ After 15 or 20 minutes, taste the rice for doneness. When the rice is about 4 minutes from being done, add the asparagus and peas, if fresh. Continue cooking, adding broth and stirring, until the rice is tender but firm, with no chalkiness in the center, and the asparagus is tender (you may not need all of the broth).

▥ Remove from the heat and stir in the peas, if previously frozen, scallions, parsley, tarragon, and 6 tablespoons of the cheese. Taste, ideally with your wine, and add more salt and/or pepper if you like.

▥ Serve the risotto hot, with the remaining 6 tablespoons of cheese crumbled on top.

smoked trout salad with endive, ricotta salata, and pickled fennel

A few years ago, a few girlfriends and I gathered at a friend's house for a spa day. We arranged two masseurs for the afternoon and, in between massages, did our nails and gabbed ourselves silly. Heaven.

Lunch was a compose-your-own salad—flavorful greens with a myriad of add-ons. This salad is inspired by our favorite toppings from that luxurious day. • **Serves 6**

    1 tablespoon Dijon mustard
    ½ teaspoon coarse kosher salt
    ½ teaspoon freshly ground black pepper
    ¾ cup white wine vinegar or champagne vinegar, divided
    ½ cup extra virgin olive oil
    ½ fennel bulb, stalks and feathery tops trimmed, halved lengthwise (into
       quarters) and sliced paper-thin
    ¼ small red onion, sliced paper-thin
    1 head escarole or chicory (about 12 ounces), cut or torn into bite-sized pieces
       (you should have about 9 cups)
    4 heads white Belgian endive, cut crosswise into ½-inch pieces
    4 heads red Belgian endive, cut crosswise into ½-inch pieces
    1 pound smoked trout (see below), skin removed, flaked into large pieces
    8 ounces ricotta salata (see below), crumbled (you should have about 1 cup)

▒ In a small bowl, combine the mustard, salt, pepper, and 4 table-spoons of the vinegar, whisking to dissolve the salt. Whisk in the olive oil. Set aside. (You can prepare the dressing up to 3 days in advance, storing it covered in the refrigerator. Return it to room temperature before serving.)

▒ In a medium bowl, combine the fennel, onion, and remaining ½ cup of vinegar. Set aside at room temperature, stirring occasionally, for 2 hours. (You can prepare the pickled fennel up to 2 days in advance, storing it covered in the refrigerator.)

▒ Drain the pickled fennel. Set aside.

▒ In a large bowl, combine the escarole, white endive, red endive, and dressing to taste. Transfer the salad to a platter or plates. Arrange the trout and ricotta salata on top, dividing both evenly. Top with a pile of the pickled fennel and serve.

NOTES You can find **smoked trout** at most specialty food stores and at many super-markets. Besides using it in this recipe, you can mix it with cream cheese to make an appetizer spread or serve it with bagels and cream cheese. **Ricotta salata** is a semihard cheese made from pressed ricotta. You can find it at cheese shops, specialty food stores, and many better supermarkets. Besides using it in this recipe, you can crumble it over other salads, casseroles, pizzas, or almost any place you would use feta. If you can't find ricotta salata, substitute a mild feta cheese.

petrale sole with lemon, capers, and croutons

My husband introduced me to petrale sole—a delicate, mildly sweet fish that, contrary to the name, is actually a flounder—and he typically mans the stove when it's prepared in our house. Often he simply flours and pan-browns it, then we add a squeeze of lemon at the table. Even that super-simple preparation is pretty perfect.

To dress it up a bit, though, we sometimes include a lemon-butter-caper sauce. And the croutons? They send this dish right over the top, soaking up a bit of the sauce and becoming crunchy and chewy at the same time. **Serves 2**

2	lemons
¼	cup all-purpose flour
¼	teaspoon white pepper, ideally freshly ground
1½	teaspoons coarse kosher salt, divided
12	ounces petrale sole, flounder, or other thin white-fleshed fish fillets
4 or 5	tablespoons unsalted butter, divided
⅔	cup croutons, homemade or store-bought
1	tablespoon drained capers
1	teaspoon chopped fresh flat-leaf parsley

Halve and squeeze 1 of the lemons to yield 1 tablespoon of juice (save the remainder of the lemon for another use). Place the juice in a small bowl. Cut the peel from the remaining lemon, then, working over the bowl with the lemon juice to catch any juices, carefully cut the segments from between the membranes, adding the segments to the bowl. Set the juice and segments aside.

In a shallow bowl, combine the flour, pepper, and 1 teaspoon of the salt. Dredge each fish fillet in the flour mixture, shaking off any excess. Sprinkle the fish with the remaining ½ teaspoon of salt.

In each of two large skillets over medium heat, melt 1 tablespoon of the butter (if your fillets are on the thick side, they might fit in one skillet—in that case use one skillet with 1 tablespoon of butter). Add the fish and cook until golden brown, 1 to 2 minutes per side. Transfer the cooked fish to a platter or plates and cover loosely with foil.

Use a paper towel to carefully wipe out one of the skillets. Return it to the stovetop over medium heat and melt the remaining 3 tablespoons of butter. Add the croutons and capers and cook, stirring, for 30 seconds. Remove from the heat and stir in the lemon juice mixture. Spoon over the fish, sprinkle with the parsley, and serve hot.

FOOD + WINE TIP This dish is super-lemony—which is why it pairs so well with super-acidic Sauvignon Blanc.

shrimp skewers with sauvignon blanc–friendly pesto

This pesto is delightfully bright and vinegary. The vinegar is what helps make the pesto, and therefore the recipe, work with typically acidic Sauvignon Blanc.

If you have leftovers, drape the pesto over a chicken breast or fish fillet and that dish, too, will pair nicely with the wine. **Serves 6**

- 12 scallions, white and light green parts only, cut into 1½-inch pieces
- 2 cups loosely packed fresh flat-leaf parsley leaves
- ¼ cup grated pecorino cheese (about 1½ ounces)
- 3 tablespoons red wine vinegar
- 2 tablespoons pine nuts, toasted (see below)
- 1 clove garlic
- 2 teaspoons coarse kosher salt, divided
- 1 teaspoon freshly ground black pepper, divided
- ¾ cup extra virgin olive oil, divided
- 2¼ pounds large, raw, peeled shrimp
- 24 cherry tomatoes
  Special equipment: 8- to 10-inch skewers, soaked in water for at least 10 minutes if they're wood or bamboo

▒ Set aside 24 of the scallion pieces. In the bowl of a food processor, combine the remaining scallions, parsley, cheese, vinegar, pine nuts, garlic, 1 teaspoon of the salt, and ½ teaspoon of the pepper and pulse to finely chop, scraping down the bowl as necessary. With the motor running, slowly add ½ cup of the olive oil and process until smooth, scraping down the bowl as necessary. (You can prepare the pesto in advance, storing it covered in the refrigerator for up to a week or in the freezer for several months. To keep refrigerated pesto nicely green, cover it with a thin layer of olive oil—or simply restir it before serving.)

▒ Thread the shrimp, cherry tomatoes, and reserved scallions onto skewers. Arrange the skewers on a rimmed baking sheet. (You can prepare the skewers up to a day in advance, storing them covered in the refrigerator.)

▒ Prepare the grill or preheat the broiler to high heat and arrange a rack about 4 inches from the heat. Brush both sides of the skewers with the remaining ¼ cup of olive oil and sprinkle with the remaining 1 teaspoon of salt and remaining ½ teaspoon of pepper. Grill or broil until the shrimp is cooked through, 1½ to 2 minutes per side. Serve the skewers hot, with the pesto drizzled on top.

NOTE To toast nuts: Spread the nuts on a rimmed baking sheet and cook in a pre-heated 350°F oven until lightly browned and fragrant, 6 to 10 minutes, depending on the type of nut and the size of the pieces. Toward the end, watch the nuts carefully—they can go from perfect to burned very quickly.

smoked lemon-soy sea bass with citrus slaw

One of the first times I ever created a noticeably perfect pairing was when I invented this dish.

I'd read an article about smoking on the grill, so my husband and I tried it out with a succulent piece of sea bass that I'd marinated in a simple concoction of lemon juice and soy sauce. To drink, we chose a type of Sauvignon Blanc called Fumé Blanc—see the Food and Wine Tip below—and when we sat down to the table and took our first bites and sips, we knew we'd stumbled onto something great.

When you visit your local fishmonger, you might find several types of sea bass—all will be great in this recipe, so ask him or her for a sustainable sea bass option. You can also substitute other firm, white-fleshed fishes such as halibut, sturgeon, or tilapia. • **Serves 6**

About 4 lemons
1 lime
1 orange
1 teaspoon coarse kosher salt, or more to taste
¼ teaspoon freshly ground black pepper, or more to taste
¼ cup canola, grapeseed, or other neutral-flavored oil
½ teaspoon sesame oil
One 10-ounce bag finely shredded cabbage or slaw mix (about 8 cups)
½ cup soy sauce
Six 6-ounce sea bass fillets, skin removed
Special equipment: wood chips for smoking (see below)

▒ Use a vegetable peeler to cut the colored part of the peel from 1 of the lemons, the lime, and half of the orange. Cut the peel crosswise into thin slices. Set the peel aside. Halve and squeeze the peeled lemon plus enough of the remaining lemons to yield ½ cup of juice (save the remaining fruit for another use).

▒ In a small bowl, combine the salt, pepper, and ¼ cup of the lemon juice, whisking to dissolve the salt. Whisk in the canola oil and sesame oil. Set aside. (You can prepare the dressing up to 3 days in advance, storing it, the sliced citrus peel, and the remaining lemon juice covered in the refrigerator.)

▒ In a large bowl, combine the cabbage, citrus peel, and dressing, gently tossing to combine. Taste, ideally with your wine, and add more lemon juice, salt, and/or pepper if you like. Set aside. (You can prepare the citrus slaw up to a day in advance, storing it covered in the refrigerator.)

▨ Combine the soy sauce and remaining ¼ cup of lemon juice in a large resealable bag. Add the fish, squeezing out as much air as possible. Set aside in the refrigerator for 1 to 2 hours, turning occasionally.

▨ Prepare one side of the grill (the side closest to your grill's smoking drawer, if it has one) to medium-high heat. Place a large handful of wood chips in a small foil pan or a foil pouch with the ends open. Place the foil pan or pouch directly onto the coals, directly over the flame, or in your grill's smoking drawer.

▨ Remove the fish from the marinade and pat it dry (discard the marinade). Lightly oil the part of the grill that doesn't have heat underneath and arrange the fish on top. If possible, open the vents below the heat source and above the fish (in a kettle-style grill, for example, position the lid so that the top vent is open over the fish). This will draw the smoke from the chips diagonally, across the fish and out the top. Smoke the fish, covered, until cooked through but still moist inside, 10 to 15 minutes, depending on the thickness. (You don't have to turn it over.) (You can also cook the fish in a stovetop smoker.)

▨ Arrange the slaw on a platter or plates. Arrange the fish on top and serve hot.

NOTE You can buy wood chips for smoking in most supermarkets and wherever charcoal and other grilling supplies are sold. Besides using them in this recipe, you can use wood chips to add smoky flavor to grilled meats, poultry, vegetables, or whatever you're cooking on the grill.

FOOD + WINE TIP Like Smoked Trout Salad with Endive, Ricotta Salata, and Pickled Fennel (page 16), this dish is especially perfect with a type of Sauvignon Blanc called Fumé Blanc. Fumé Blanc is often aged in oak, which helps it pair with smoky dishes.

herbed goat cheese–stuffed chicken breasts on a spring herb salad

The light, bright flavors of spring are laced throughout this delicious, and pretty, dish.

You'll notice that the recipe calls for, ideally, skin-on chicken breasts. It's just because they're tastier, they brown up better, and the crispness adds a nice texture. But they can be hard to find. So don't sweat it. If you can't find them—or if you'd rather save a few calories—just use readily available skinless ones. • **Serves 4**

    1 ruby grapefruit
    2 tablespoons white or golden balsamic vinegar (see below)
1½ teaspoons coarse kosher salt, divided, or more to taste
   ½ teaspoon freshly ground black pepper, divided, or more to taste
   ¼ cup extra virgin olive oil, divided
    1 large or 2 small heads butter lettuce, cut or torn into bite-sized pieces (you should have about 6 cups)
   ½ cup coarsely chopped fresh chives (½-inch pieces), plus 1 teaspoon finely chopped fresh chives (⅛-inch pieces)
   ½ cup fresh cilantro leaves, plus 1 teaspoon chopped fresh cilantro
   ½ cup fresh flat-leaf parsley leaves, plus 1 teaspoon chopped fresh flat-leaf parsley
   ½ cup fresh mint leaves, plus 1 teaspoon chopped fresh mint
   ½ cup chèvre (spreadable goat cheese) (about 4 ounces)
    4 large boneless chicken breasts (1¾ to 2 pounds), ideally skin-on

▥ Finely grate the zest from the grapefruit (you should have about 1½ teaspoons packed). Set aside.

▥ Halve the grapefruit and squeeze it to yield 1 tablespoon of juice (save the remaining grapefruit for another use). In a small bowl, combine the grapefruit juice, vinegar, ½ teaspoon of the salt, and half of the grapefruit zest, whisking to dissolve the salt. Whisk in 2 tablespoons of the olive oil. Set aside. (You can prepare the dressing up to 3 days in advance, storing it and the remaining zest covered in the refrigerator. Return the dressing to room temperature before serving.)

▥ In a large bowl, combine the lettuce, coarsely chopped chives, cilantro leaves, parsley leaves, and mint leaves. Set aside in the refrigerator.

▥ In a medium bowl, combine the cheese, finely chopped chives, chopped cilantro, chopped parsley, chopped mint, remaining grapefruit zest, ½ teaspoon of the remaining salt, and ¼ teaspoon of the pepper. Set aside. (You can prepare the salad and the cheese stuffing up to a day in advance, storing them covered in the refrigerator.)

▦ Remove the tenders, if any, from the chicken breasts (save them for another use). Use a small, sharp knife to carefully cut into the thickest part of the side of each breast, forming a pocket that extends to within about ¾ inch from all the edges of the breast, with about a 1½-inch opening. Use a small spoon to stuff about 2 tablespoons of the cheese mixture into each breast, distributing it evenly within the pocket and securing the opening with a wooden toothpick. Sprinkle both sides of the chicken with the remaining ½ teaspoon of salt and remaining ¼ teaspoon of pepper.

▦ In a large skillet over medium heat, warm the remaining 2 table-spoons of olive oil. Add the chicken, skin side down, and cook until well browned and cooked through, about 6 minutes per side. Transfer the chicken to a platter or plate and let it rest, loosely covered with foil, for 5 minutes.

▦ Meanwhile, add the dressing to the salad, tossing to combine. Taste, ideally with your wine, and add more salt and/or pepper if you like.

▦ Arrange the salad on a platter or plates. Top with the chicken and serve hot, with any accumulated juices drizzled on top. (Warn your guests about the toothpicks.)

> **NOTE** You could say that **white or golden balsamic vinegar** is to balsamic vinegar as white grape juice is to grape juice—they're similar, but the white version is lighter and fruitier. You can find white or golden balsamic in most supermarkets and wherever regular balsamic is sold. Besides using it in this recipe, you can use it in Pan-Seared Rosemary Rainbow Trout with Cherry Tomato Relish (page 38), Classic Cobb Salad (page 39), Grilled Grouper with 'Cress and 'Cado Relish (page 49), Grilled Chicken with Marinated Peppers (page 51), and Honey-Orange Lamb Chops (page 99). You can also use it in many of your favorite salad dressings.

acidity + acidity = less acidity

It's totally contrary to logic that adding more of something to a pairing will decrease your overall experience of it, but that's what happens in food and wine pairing—more acidity in the food will decrease your experience of acidity in the wine, more sweetness in the food will decrease your experience of sweetness in the wine, more bitterness in the food will decrease your experience of bitterness, or tannins, in the wine. But because it works that way, acidic foods are your best bet for acidic Sauvignon Blanc.

By acidic foods, I mean foods with bright ingredients—vinegar, lemon juice, buttermilk, and sour cream, to name a few. More of any of them will usually improve a Sauvignon Blanc pairing.

chicken paillards with baby artichokes, garlic, and lemon

When I lived in New York City, my neighborhood had an Italian restaurant whose name I unfortunately can't remember. What I've never been able to forget, however, is my favorite dish there—thinly pounded chicken breasts and fresh baby artichokes in a silky sauce loaded with lemon juice and garlic. I haven't had anything like it before or since, and so, still craving it after all these years, I finally replicated it in my own kitchen with this recipe.

The dish is best with fresh baby artichokes—which I highly recommend trying if you've never cooked with them—but they're sometimes hard to find out of season. Other times of year, the dish is 98 percent as good with frozen artichoke hearts. **Serves 4**

    1 pound fresh baby artichokes (about 8) or one 8- to 10-ounce package
      frozen artichoke hearts, thawed
    2 or 3 tablespoons fresh lemon juice (about 2 lemons), divided, or more to taste
    4 large boneless, skinless chicken breasts (1¾ to 2 pounds)
  ⅓ cup all-purpose flour
2½ teaspoons coarse kosher salt, divided, or more to taste
    1 teaspoon freshly ground black pepper, divided, or more to taste
  ¼ cup extra virgin olive oil, divided
    6 cloves garlic, thinly sliced
  ½ cup reduced-sodium chicken broth
1½ teaspoons chopped fresh thyme
    2 tablespoons (¼ stick) unsalted butter

▦ If using fresh artichokes, fill a large bowl with 4 cups of cold water and add 1 tablespoon of the lemon juice. Working with 1 artichoke at a time, snap off the leaves until you reach leaves that are about three-quarters yellow and one-quarter green. Trim the top, removing the green part of the leaves. Trim the stem, then trim around the sides of the stem, removing the dark green parts and creating a stubby cone shape at the base of the artichoke. Cut the artichoke lengthwise into ⅛-inch slices, then transfer the slices to the lemon water to help prevent them from browning. Repeat with the remaining artichokes. Set aside. (You can prepare the artichokes up to a day in advance, storing them in the lemon water, covered, in the refrigerator.)

▦ Remove the tenders, if any, from the chicken breasts (save them for another use). Arrange the breasts on a work surface and use a meat pounder to pound them to a uniform thickness, between ¼ and ½ inch.

▒ In a shallow bowl, combine the flour, 1½ teaspoons of the salt, and ½ teaspoon of the pepper. Dredge each chicken breast in the flour mixture, shaking off any excess. Sprinkle the chicken with ½ teaspoon of the remaining salt and ¼ teaspoon of the remaining pepper. Set aside.

▒ If using fresh artichokes, drain them.

▒ In a large skillet over medium-high heat, warm 2 tablespoons of the olive oil. Add the artichokes, garlic, remaining ½ teaspoon of salt, and remaining ¼ teaspoon of pepper. Cook, stirring occasionally, until the artichokes begin to brown, 2 to 3 minutes for fresh artichokes or 30 to 60 seconds for previously frozen. Transfer the artichoke mixture to a plate or bowl and set aside.

▒ Return the skillet to medium-high heat and warm the remaining 2 tablespoons of olive oil. Add the chicken and cook until browned, about 2 minutes per side. Transfer the chicken to a plate and set aside.

▒ Return the skillet to medium-high heat and add the broth, thyme, and remaining 2 tablespoons of lemon juice, scraping up any browned bits on the bottom of the skillet. Return the chicken and artichokes to the skillet, along with any accumulated juices, nestling the chicken into the liquid. Bring to a boil, reduce to a simmer, cover, and cook until the chicken is cooked through and the artichokes are tender, 5 to 6 minutes. Transfer the chicken to a platter or plates.

▒ Remove the skillet from the heat and add the butter, stirring until it melts. Taste the artichokes and sauce, ideally with your wine, and add more salt, pepper, and/or lemon juice if you like. Spoon the artichokes and sauce over the chicken and serve hot.

FOOD + WINE TIP This recipe also works with Pinot Grigio.

penne with chicken, asparagus, and pancetta

This easy pasta is simple enough for a weeknight, yet indulgent enough for company. It's both bright tasting and rich—Sauvignon Blanc complements the flavors and counterbalances the creaminess.

Nine times out of ten, when cooking pasta, I'd say to make the water well salted, using one tablespoon of coarse kosher salt per quart. In this dish, though, there's already a good amount of salt in the pancetta and cheeses. So season the pasta water only half as much. **Serves 4 to 6**

    8 ounces penne pasta
   12 ounces asparagus (about ¾ of a standard-sized bunch), trimmed and cut
      into 1-inch pieces (you should have about 2 cups)
    8 thin slices pancetta (about 4 ounces) (see below), cut into ¼-inch strips
    2 large boneless, skinless chicken breasts (about 1 pound), cut into ¼-inch slices
    ½ cup crème fraîche
    ⅓ cup milk (low-fat is okay)
    ¼ cup basil pesto, homemade or store-bought
    ¼ cup grated pecorino cheese (about 1½ ounces), or more to taste

▒ In a large pot of boiling, mildly salted water (1½ teaspoons of coarse kosher salt per quart), cook the pasta according to package directions. Stir in the asparagus 3 minutes before the pasta is al dente.

▒ While the pasta is cooking, in a large skillet over medium heat, cook the pancetta, stirring occasionally, until golden, about 4 minutes. Use a slotted spoon to transfer the pancetta to a bowl or plate. Increase the heat to high, add the chicken to the skillet, and cook, stirring occasionally, until cooked through, 2 to 3 minutes. Add the crème fraîche and milk and cook, stirring, until the mixture returns to a boil. Remove from the heat and stir in the pesto, cheese, and pancetta. Set aside, covered, until the pasta is done.

▒ Drain the pasta and immediately add it to the skillet, tossing to coat. Serve the pasta hot, topped with additional cheese, if you like.

NOTE Pancetta is an Italian bacon that comes shaped into a sliceable, sausage-like roll. Because it's not smoked, it has a slightly different flavor than American bacon. Pancetta is available at the deli counter of most major supermarkets, but if you can't find it, substitute bacon, cut into ¼-inch strips. Besides using it in this recipe, you can use pancetta in Chicken Cocoa Vin (page 136) and almost any place that you'd use bacon.

pinot grigio

There's a restaurant in Napa, a glorified burger joint really, called Gott's Roadside Tray Gourmet (formerly Taylor's Refresher). It's one of my favorite places to treat myself to a lunch of chicken Caesar salad and a glass of Pinot Grigio, a killer combination.

Pinot Grigio is similar to Sauvignon Blanc in that it's crisp and citrusy. But Pinot Grigio tends to be a little less acidic, lending itself to slightly softer dishes, and it tends to have a little more body, lending itself to slightly heavier dishes.

That said, in terms of food and wine pairing, the two are very similar. Many of the recipes in this chapter will also work with Sauvignon Blanc—and vice versa.

pinot grigio by another name

• **Pinot Gris.** This is the name for the same grape in France, where it's widely grown in Alsace. Because the French don't label their wines by varietal name, you're unlikely to see "Pinot Gris" on a French wine bottle, but a non-French producer might use the term, presumably to indicate the wine is made in a French style versus an Italian one.

pairing with pinot grigio

Although there are, of course, nuances to Pinot Grigio, the most important factors in food and wine pairing aren't a wine's nuances, but its broad strokes. If you learn a wine's overall characteristics and combine that information with the General Pairing Tips (page 8), you'll have a near-perfect pairing every time.

Broad characteristics:
• dry (not sweet)
• medium-high in acidity, crispness, or brightness
• no or very low tannins
• light to medium weight
• medium intensity

Pairs well with dishes that are:
• not sweet
• medium-high in acidity, crispness, or brightness
• light to medium weight
• medium intensity

(Because the wine has no or very low tannins, they're not a factor.)
For example, Italian antipasto, seafood pasta with white wine sauce, or salad with ranch or buttermilk dressing.

fine-tuning

As with Sauvignon Blanc, a little more acid and/or salt will almost always help a food pair with typically bright Pinot Grigio. Have some form of each on hand for fine-tuning dishes to your particular bottle.

And as with Sauvignon Blanc, because Pinot Grigio is a light white wine, use similarly lighter, whiter acids, like lemon juice, white wine or champagne vinegar, white or golden balsamic vinegar, buttermilk, and even sour cream. Sometimes simply adding some lemon zest or a bright cheese, like feta, will take a Pinot Grigio pairing from good to great.

other nuances

Once you have a pairing that's working on the basis of sweetness, acidity, weight, and intensity, you can start playing with subtler nuances.

Some of the subtle flavors that you might find in a Pinot Grigio include citrus, green apple, pear, stone fruits, floral notes, and minerality. So it works to add those flavors, or foods that complement them, to your dishes.

Being the quintessential Italian white wine, Pinot Grigio also tends to work with lighter, typically northern Italian dishes and ingredients.

other thoughts

Some foods that are considered classic pairings with Pinot Grigio are goat and sheep cheeses, fish and shellfish, chicken, and pasta (especially with white sauces, wine sauces, and/or seafood).

savory goat cheese cheesecake with zucchini-lemon topping

Almost a quiche, not quite a mousse, this cheesecake is somewhere in between, silky and smooth yet divinely light. The zucchini topping brings added taste, texture, and a burst of bright lemon flavor. Perhaps best of all, the finished dish feels special, but it's not hard to make.

Try it for brunch, lunch, or a light dinner, accompanied by a big salad, a hunk of good bread, and of course, a glass of Pinot Grigio.

Serves 8 to 10

FOR THE CRUST
1 cup plain breadcrumbs
6 tablespoons (¾ stick) unsalted butter, melted
¼ cup grated Parmesan cheese (about 1½ ounces)

FOR THE FILLING
1½ cups chèvre (spreadable goat cheese) (about 12 ounces), room temperature
4 large eggs, room temperature
12 ounces cream cheese, cut into 4 to 6 pieces, room temperature
1 cup sour cream, room temperature
4 teaspoons cornstarch
2 teaspoons coarse kosher salt
¼ teaspoon white pepper, ideally freshly ground
¼ cup chopped fresh chives

FOR THE TOPPING
2 tablespoons extra virgin olive oil
12 ounces zucchini (2 to 3 medium), shredded (you should have about 2¾ cups)
½ onion, halved lengthwise (into quarters) and thinly sliced
1 lemon, quartered lengthwise and thinly sliced (peel and all)
2 teaspoons coarse kosher salt, or more to taste
¼ cup coarsely chopped fresh flat-leaf parsley
2 tablespoons chopped fresh chives

Special equipment: 9-inch springform pan

■ Preheat the oven to 350°F. Wrap a 9-inch springform pan with foil, covering the bottom and up the sides, so that it's watertight. Set aside.

■ To make the crust: In a medium bowl, combine the breadcrumbs, butter, and Parmesan, mixing to thoroughly combine. Press the mixture into the bottom and 1½ to 2 inches up the sides of the prepared springform pan. Set aside in the refrigerator.

▓ To make the filling: In the bowl of an electric mixer fitted with a paddle attachment, beat the goat cheese and eggs on medium speed until combined. Gradually add the cream cheese, beating until combined. Add the sour cream, cornstarch, salt, and pepper, beating just until smooth. Stir in the chives. Pour the filling into the crust, spreading it evenly, and place the springform pan in a larger baking pan. Pour enough hot water into the larger pan so that the water is 1 inch deep. Bake until the middle of the cheesecake is set, about an hour.

▓ Remove the cheesecake from the water and immediately run a knife around the edges to release it from the pan. Transfer the pan to a wire rack and allow to cool.

▓ Meanwhile, make the topping: In a medium saucepan over medium-high heat, warm the olive oil. Add the zucchini and onion and cook, stirring occasionally, until the vegetables are tender, about 5 minutes. Add the lemon, salt, and ⅓ cup water and bring to a boil. Reduce to a simmer, cover, and cook, stirring occasionally, until the lemon peel is very tender and the liquid is almost entirely absorbed, about 15 minutes. Remove from the heat and stir in the parsley and chives. Taste, ideally with your wine, and add more salt if you like. (You can prepare the cheesecake and the topping up to 2 days in advance. Cool both thoroughly, then store them covered in the refrigerator. Return them to room temperature, or slightly rewarm the topping, before serving.)

▓ Spread the topping mixture evenly over the cheesecake. Unmold the cheesecake from the pan. Slice and serve warm or room temperature.

FOOD + WINE TIP Goat cheese and Sauvignon Blanc is considered a classic pairing—but it's great with Pinot Grigio as well.

fresh tomato and herb fettuccine

This beautifully simple pasta is a great way to enjoy home-grown or farmer's market tomatoes. It's one of those dishes that's so basic, using the best ingredients will really make a difference. **Serves 4**

   2 ounces Parmesan cheese
  12 ounces fettuccine pasta
  ⅓ cup plus ¼ cup extra virgin olive oil, divided
   6 shallots, thinly sliced
   4 cloves garlic, thinly sliced
   4 pounds tomatoes, preferably heirloom and a combination of colors, cored, seeded, and cut into ¾-inch dice (you should have about 6½ cups)
  ½ cup thinly sliced fresh basil
  1½ teaspoons coarse kosher salt
  ½ teaspoon freshly ground black pepper

▦ Use a vegetable peeler to cut the cheese into thick shaves (you should have about ⅔ cup). (You can shave the cheese up to a day in advance, storing it covered in the refrigerator.)

▦ In a large pot of boiling, well-salted water (1 tablespoon of coarse kosher salt per quart), cook the pasta according to package directions.

▦ Meanwhile, in a large skillet over medium-high heat, warm ⅓ cup of the olive oil. Add the shallots and cook, stirring occasionally, for 5 minutes. Add the garlic and cook, stirring occasionally, until the shallots and garlic are tender, about 2 minutes. Reduce the heat to medium and add the tomatoes, basil, salt, and pepper. Cook, stirring, until the tomatoes are heated through, about 2 minutes. Remove the skillet from the heat.

▦ Drain the pasta and transfer it to a serving bowl or to individual bowls. Top with the tomato mixture, drizzle with the remaining ¼ cup of olive oil, and sprinkle with the cheese. Serve hot.

how to cook with wine

1 Cook with red when a recipe calls for red, white when a recipe calls for white, dry (not sweet) when a recipe calls for dry, and sweet when a recipe calls for sweet. Beyond that, the particular type of, say, dry red wine that you use isn't critical.

2 Don't cook with a wine that you wouldn't drink. So if you're happy to drink inexpensive wine, it's fine for cooking. If you're not, it's not. Using an expensive bottle also doesn't make sense. So cook with something in between—whatever that means for you.

3 Know that when you add wine to a dish, essentially what you're adding is a mild acid, which, per Fine-Tuning Tip 1 (page 9), will decrease your experience of acid and tannins and increase your experience of fruit or sweetness in the wine you pair with it.

white wine seafood pasta

If I'm at a restaurant and there's a seafood pasta on the menu, I almost always order it. I just love the combination of briny fish and shellfish, a light wine-soused sauce, and silky noodles.

But there's no need to restrict enjoyment of this dish to a restaurant. It's really easy to make at home and comes together in a snap. The most difficult part is simply assembling the ingredients, which shouldn't be a problem if you have a good fishmonger in your midst.

Serves 4

- 12 ounces linguine pasta
- 3 tablespoons extra virgin olive oil
- 2 cloves garlic, thinly sliced
- ½ teaspoon dried crushed red pepper flakes
- 1 tablespoon tomato paste
- ½ pound mussels, scrubbed and debearded
- ⅓ cup bottled clam juice
- 1 teaspoon coarse kosher salt, or more to taste
- ½ cup Pinot Grigio, or other dry white wine, divided
- ½ pound clams, scrubbed
- ½ pound firm white-fleshed fish fillets, such as halibut, sturgeon, or tilapia, or a combination, skin removed, cut into 1-inch pieces
- ½ pound large, raw, peeled shrimp, preferably tail on
- 4 tablespoons (½ stick) unsalted butter, cut into 3 or 4 pieces
- 2 tablespoons chopped fresh flat-leaf parsley

In a large pot of boiling, well-salted water (1 tablespoon of coarse kosher salt per quart), cook the pasta according to package directions.

Meanwhile, in a large skillet over medium-high heat, warm the olive oil. Add the garlic and red pepper flakes and cook, stirring occasionally, for 30 seconds. Add the tomato paste and cook, stirring, for 30 seconds. Stir in the mussels, clam juice, salt, and ¼ cup of the wine and bring to a boil. Reduce to a simmer, cover, and cook for 2 minutes. Stir in the clams, fish, and shrimp. Increase the heat to medium-high and return to a boil. Reduce to a simmer, recover, and cook until the mussels and clams are open and the fish and shrimp are cooked through, 4 to 6 minutes (discard any mussels or clams that don't open).

Drain the pasta and transfer it to a serving bowl or to individual bowls. Use a slotted spoon to arrange the seafood on top, dividing it evenly. Add the butter and remaining ¼ cup of wine to the sauce in the skillet and stir until the butter melts. Taste, ideally with your wine, and add more salt if you like.

Spoon the sauce over the seafood and pasta, sprinkle the parsley on top, and serve hot.

fish "burgers" with minted napa cabbage slaw

My friend Carole introduced me to a version of this slaw eons ago, and I've loved it ever since. Napa cabbage has a juiciness, a refreshing crunch that regular cabbage doesn't—which helps the slaw nicely complement a similarly light and refreshing piece of fish. **Serves 6**

    3 tablespoons white wine vinegar or champagne vinegar, or more to taste
    ½ shallot, finely diced
    ¼ teaspoon sugar
    2½ teaspoons coarse kosher salt, divided, or more to taste
    1¼ teaspoons freshly ground black pepper, divided, or more to taste
    5 tablespoons canola, grapeseed, or other neutral-flavored oil, divided
    ½ pound napa cabbage (¼ medium head), cored and cut into ¼-inch shreds
      (you should have about 3 cups)
    ¼ cup crumbled blue cheese (about 1 ounce)
    1 tablespoon chopped fresh mint
      Six 6-ounce firm white-fleshed fish fillets, such as halibut, sturgeon, or tilapia,
      about ¾ inch thick, skin removed
    6 hamburger buns or kaiser rolls, split horizontally

In a small bowl, combine the vinegar, shallot, sugar, ½ teaspoon of the salt, and ¼ teaspoon of the pepper, whisking to dissolve the sugar and salt. Whisk in 3 tablespoons of the oil. Set aside. (You can prepare the dressing up to 3 days in advance, storing it covered in the refrigerator.)

In a large bowl, combine the cabbage, cheese, and mint. (You can prepare the undressed slaw up to 4 hours in advance, storing it covered in the refrigerator.)

Add the dressing to the slaw mixture, gently tossing to combine. Taste, ideally with your wine, and add more vinegar, salt, and/or pepper if you like. Set aside.

Prepare the grill to medium-high heat. Brush both sides of the fish with the remaining 2 tablespoons of oil and sprinkle with the remaining 2 teaspoons of salt and remaining 1 teaspoon of pepper. Grill until cooked through, about 3 minutes per side. During the last minute, place the buns on the grill, cut side down, to lightly toast.

Place the fish fillets on the bottom halves of the buns. Top with the slaw and the top halves of the buns and serve.

FOOD + WINE TIP Although the cabbage is light and refreshing, the dish overall is just on the edge of being rich enough to merit a Chardonnay. To tip the scales in that direction, spread some mayo on the buns or increase the amount of blue cheese in the slaw. Or both!

aniseed-crusted ahi with edamame three-bean salad

This dish starts with the familiar flavors of seared tuna and three-bean salad, then adds flavorful interest and dimension with aniseed, edamame, and fresh herbs. • **Serves 4**

   3 tablespoons red wine vinegar, or more to taste
   1 clove garlic, pressed through a garlic press or minced
   ¾ teaspoon Dijon mustard
   2 teaspoons coarse kosher salt, divided, or more to taste
   ¾ teaspoon freshly ground black pepper, divided, or more to taste
   2 tablespoons extra virgin olive oil
   ½ cup corn kernels, fresh or frozen, thawed if frozen
   ½ cup shelled edamame beans, thawed if frozen
      One 8.75-ounce can red kidney beans, drained and rinsed
      One 8.75-ounce can garbanzo beans, drained and rinsed
   ½ green bell pepper, cored, seeded, and cut into ¼-inch dice
   2 scallions, white and light green parts only, thinly sliced
   1 tablespoon chopped fresh flat-leaf parsley
   1 tablespoon chopped fresh dill
   4 teaspoons aniseed
 1½ to 2 pounds ahi tuna steaks, about 1½ inches thick, skin removed
   2 tablespoons safflower, sunflower, peanut, or other high-heat cooking oil

In a small bowl, combine the vinegar, garlic, mustard, 1 teaspoon of the salt, and ¼ teaspoon of the black pepper, whisking to dissolve the salt. Whisk in the olive oil. Set aside. (You can prepare the dressing up to 3 days in advance, storing it covered in the refrigerator.)

In a medium bowl, combine the corn, edamame, kidney beans, garbanzo beans, bell pepper, scallions, parsley, and dill. Add the dressing, gently tossing to combine. Taste, ideally with your wine, and add more vinegar, salt, and/or black pepper if you like. Set aside. (You can prepare the three-bean salad up to a day in advance, storing it covered in the refrigerator.)

In a small bowl, combine the aniseed, remaining 1 teaspoon of salt, and remaining ½ teaspoon of black pepper. Press the aniseed mixture evenly over one side of the tuna.

In a large skillet over medium-high heat, warm the safflower oil. Add the tuna, crusted side down, and cook until well seared, about 3 minutes per side for medium rare. Transfer the tuna to a cutting board and let it rest, loosely covered with foil, for 5 minutes.

Meanwhile, arrange the three-bean salad on a platter or plates.

Cut the tuna into ½-inch slices, arrange it on top of or on the side of the salad, and serve.

pan-seared rosemary rainbow trout with cherry tomato relish

Quick-cooking, flavorful, and readily available, rainbow trout is a great seafood option. This particular preparation can be ready in about fifteen minutes—and is especially pretty if you use a medley of cherry tomato shapes and colors.

On the side, try steamed potatoes or green beans. **Serves 4**

2 cups halved cherry tomatoes, ideally a combination of colors and shapes
1 large shallot, finely diced
3 tablespoons white or golden balsamic vinegar (see note on page 23)
2 teaspoons chopped fresh rosemary, plus 8 sprigs
3 tablespoons plus 4 teaspoons extra virgin olive oil, divided
1½ teaspoons coarse kosher salt, divided
½ teaspoon freshly ground black pepper, divided
Four 10- to 12-ounce whole rainbow trout, heads and tails removed if you'd like (see below)

In a medium bowl, combine the cherry tomatoes, shallot, vinegar, chopped rosemary, 4 teaspoons of the olive oil, ½ teaspoon of the salt, and ¼ teaspoon of the pepper. Set aside. (You can prepare the relish up to 2 hours in advance, storing it covered at room temperature.)

Sprinkle the trout inside and out with the remaining 1 teaspoon of salt and remaining ¼ teaspoon of pepper. Stuff each trout with 2 sprigs of the rosemary. In each of 2 large skillets over medium-high heat, warm 1½ tablespoons of the remaining olive oil. Add the trout and cook until well browned and barely opaque, about 3½ minutes per side.

Serve hot, with the tomato relish on top.

NOTE Sometimes a whole rainbow trout will be boneless, and sometimes it won't. No matter which kind your local fishmonger has, this recipe will work, using the same cooking times.

classic cobb salad

There's a reason this salad—reportedly invented at Hollywood's Brown Derby restaurant and definitely popularized by it—is still enjoyed over seventy years later. It's a perfect combination of light and rich, salty and savory, refreshing and intense. A bright-yet-creamy dressing makes it the perfect foil for Pinot Grigio. **Serves 4**

½ cup mayonnaise
¼ cup white or golden balsamic vinegar (see note on page 23)
1 teaspoon Dijon mustard
½ teaspoon coarse kosher salt
¼ teaspoon freshly ground black pepper
1 large or 2 small boneless, skinless chicken breasts (about 12 ounces)
1 head butter lettuce, cut or torn into bite-sized pieces (you should have 8 or 9 cups)
8 thick slices crisp-cooked bacon, crumbled or chopped
1 large or 2 small avocados, peeled, pitted, and cut into ½-inch dice
2 hard-cooked eggs, peeled, halved, and chopped
1 cup halved cherry tomatoes
¾ cup crumbled blue cheese (about 3 ounces)
½ small red onion, cut into ¼-inch dice

In a small bowl, combine the mayonnaise, vinegar, mustard, salt, and pepper, whisking to dissolve the salt. Set aside. (You can prepare the dressing up to 3 days in advance, storing it covered in the refrigerator.)

In a medium saucepan of barely simmering, well-salted water (1 tablespoon of coarse kosher salt per quart), poach the chicken, uncovered, for 6 minutes. Remove from the heat and let it stand, covered, until the chicken is cooked through, 10 to 12 minutes. Transfer the chicken to a cutting board to cool completely, then cut it into ½-inch dice. (You can prepare the chicken up to 2 days in advance, storing it covered in the refrigerator.)

Arrange the lettuce on a platter or plates. Arrange the chicken, bacon, avocados, eggs, cherry tomatoes, and cheese on top, dividing them evenly. Sprinkle with the onion, drizzle with the dressing, and serve.

honey-mustard pork tenderloin with roasted carrots and parsnips

A pork tenderloin is a great weeknight roast because it cooks so quickly. In this recipe it gets slathered with a simple yet flavorful Dijon mustard sauce and served with a tasty combination of carrots and parsnips. **Serves 6**

   1 pound parsnips, cut into ½-inch dice (you should have about 3 cups)
  12 ounces carrots, cut into ½-inch dice (you should have about 2 cups)
  ¼ cup extra virgin olive oil
  2 teaspoons coarse kosher salt
  ⅓ cup Dijon mustard
  2 tablespoons honey
  1 tablespoon mustard seeds, preferably brown
     Two 1-pound pork tenderloins, trimmed and ideally brined (see page 81)

▨ Preheat the oven to 450°F. Arrange one rack in the bottom third of the oven and another in the middle.

▨ In a medium bowl, combine the parsnips, carrots, olive oil, and salt, tossing to coat. Spread the mixture on a large, rimmed baking sheet. Set aside.

▨ In a small bowl, combine the mustard and honey. Spread the mixture all over the pork. Place the pork on a rack in a 9 x 13-inch baking pan and pour any remaining mustard mixture over the top. Sprinkle the top of the tenderloins with the mustard seeds. Add about ¼ inch of water to the bottom of the pan.

▨ Place the pork on the middle rack and roast for 10 minutes.

▨ Place the carrots and parsnips on the bottom rack and continue roasting until an internal thermometer in the pork reads 140°F for medium rare, 15 to 20 minutes. Transfer the pork to a cutting board and let it rest, loosely covered with foil, for 10 minutes. (It will continue to cook, reaching an internal temperature of about 150°F.)

▨ Meanwhile, toss the carrots and parsnips and continue roasting until tender, about 10 minutes.

▨ Slice the pork on an angle and arrange on a platter or plates. Drizzle with any accumulated juices, spoon the carrots and parsnips on top, and serve hot.

FOOD + WINE TIP You could argue that pork is a little heavy for a light wine like Pinot Grigio, yet the pairing works. That's because the tenderloin, lacking a lot of fat, is one of the lightest cuts of pork. It also works because of the mustard's brightness.

chardonnay

Chardonnay is kind of the Coke of wines. It's popular. It's easy to drink. And it goes with a lot of great foods.

That popularity, however, has led some to look down on Chardonnay. I think the logic is that if it's that popular, it couldn't possibly be cool.

But I think Chardonnay is totally cool. Because I love Brie and avocados and roast chicken and crab—and similarly rich and weighty foods—and a rich, weighty wine like Chardonnay is perfect for pairing with them.

That said, styles of Chardonnay can vary widely, from crisp and refreshing to buttery and soft—and everything in between. But my experience is that as long as you match Chardonnay's weight with richness in your food, it doesn't matter what style of Chardonnay you serve. The buttery ones will complement creamy flavors while the crisper ones will provide contrast and help cleanse your palate between bites.

Cool.

chardonnay by another name

• **Burgundy, White Burgundy.** As with other French wines, these French Chardonnays are labeled with the name of the area they're from. They might have the general area name Burgundy, or names of subregions within Burgundy (Mâcon or Mâconnais, for example). Basically, any white wine from Burgundy will be made from the Chardonnay grape. • **Chablis.** Like Mâconnais, this is also an area in Burgundy, but one where winemakers produce Chardonnays with a characteristically crisp, steely, even mineral-y style.

pairing with chardonnay

Although there are, of course, nuances to Chardonnay, the most important factors in food and wine pairing aren't a wine's nuances, but its broad strokes. If you learn a wine's overall characteristics and combine that information with the General Pairing Tips (page 8), you'll have a near-perfect pairing every time.

Broad characteristics:
- dry (not sweet)
- low to medium-high in acidity, crispness, or brightness
- no or very low tannins
- medium to heavy weight
- medium to strong intensity

Pairs well with dishes that are:

- not sweet
- low to medium-high in acidity, crispness, or brightness
- medium to heavy weight
- medium to strong intensity

(Because the wine has no or very low tannins, they're not a factor.)
For example, crackers and Brie, garlic roasted chicken, or French onion soup.

But overall, the most important factor in pairing foods with Chardonnay is the weight—pair rich foods with this rich wine.

fine-tuning

It seems like every single Chardonnay pairing is better with more cream, more mayonnaise, more cheese, more avocado.

If you know your Chardonnay is on the crisper side, your creamy elements can stand some acidity in them. For example, use buttermilk, sour cream, and even blue cheese.

If you know your Chardonnay is on the buttery side, keep your creamy elements blander. For example, use butter, mayonnaise, avocado, and buttery cheeses like Brie.

And if you don't know which kind of Chardonnay you've got, don't worry about it.

other nuances

Once you have a pairing that's working on the basis of sweetness, acidity, weight, and intensity, you can start playing with subtler nuances.

Some of the subtle flavors that you might find in a Chardonnay include apple, pear, stone fruits, tropical fruits, citrus, melon, toast, butterscotch, vanilla, nuts, and minerality. So it works to add those flavors, or foods that complement them, to your dishes.

other thoughts

Some foods that are considered classic pairings with Chardonnay are creamy cheeses, chicken (especially grilled or roasted), richer fish and shellfish (especially crab and lobster), veal, and anything with butter, cream, or a buttery/creamy sauce.

chanterelle and gruyère bread pudding

Indulgent, delicious, and ooey-gooey satisfying—despite being pretty simple—this dish has it all. Serve it with a big green salad and you've got the makings for a wonderful lunch, brunch, or light dinner.

This recipe will also serve eight to ten as a side dish—it would be great with roasted meats, poultry, or even fish. • **Serves 6**

3 cups milk (low-fat is okay)
1½ teaspoons chopped fresh rosemary
1 teaspoon chopped fresh thyme
1 teaspoon chopped fresh sage
¼ teaspoon freshly ground black pepper
4 tablespoons (½ stick) unsalted butter, plus more for buttering the pan
6 ounces chanterelle mushrooms, coarsely sliced (you should have about 2½ cups)
1½ teaspoons coarse kosher salt
5 large eggs
12 ounces crusty artisan French or Italian bread, with crusts, cut or torn into ¾-inch pieces (you should have about 12 cups)
8 ounces Gruyère cheese, shredded (you should have about 3 cups)
Optional special equipment: six 1½-cup soufflé molds or ramekins

▨ Butter a 2-quart casserole dish or six 1½-cup soufflé molds or ramekins. If using 6 molds, arrange them on a rimmed baking sheet. Set aside.

▨ In a medium saucepan over medium-high heat, combine the milk, rosemary, thyme, sage, and pepper and heat until just shy of simmering. Remove from the heat and set aside to cool slightly.

▨ Meanwhile, in a large skillet over medium heat, melt the butter. Add the mushrooms and salt and cook, stirring occasionally, until the mushrooms are tender, 4 to 5 minutes. Remove from the heat and set aside.

▨ In a large bowl, whisk the eggs. Whisk in the cooled milk mixture. Add the bread, cheese, and mushroom mixture, stirring until well combined. Set aside for 15 minutes, gently stirring occasionally, for the bread to absorb the liquid.

▨ Meanwhile, preheat the oven to 375°F.

▨ Pour the entire mixture into the prepared casserole dish or soufflé molds. Bake until golden brown, 30 to 35 minutes. Serve hot.

FOOD + WINE TIP Some Chardonnays have more of a buttery quality, and some are more crisp. Either style works with a rich dish like this one—the buttery wines echo the richness and the crisper ones provide a palate-cleansing contrast.

crème fraîche fettuccine alfredo with cauliflower

Adding crème fraîche to a traditional Alfredo sauce does two things. It gives the dish a delectably contemporary twist. But more importantly, it helps match the dish to the wine, with the crème fraîche contributing both richness and brightness, mimicking those characteristics in Chardonnay. **Serves 4**

12 ounces fettuccine pasta
3 cups small cauliflower florets
6 tablespoons (¾ stick) unsalted butter
1 cup crème fraîche
1 cup heavy whipping cream
¾ cup grated Parmesan cheese (4 to 5 ounces), plus more for serving
1 teaspoon coarse kosher salt, plus more to taste
½ teaspoon white pepper, ideally freshly ground, plus more to taste
4 thin slices prosciutto (about 2 ounces), cut crosswise into ¼-inch strips (optional)

In a large pot of boiling, well-salted water (1 tablespoon of coarse kosher salt per quart), cook the pasta according to package directions. Stir in the cauliflower 4 minutes before the pasta is al dente.

While the pasta is cooking, in a small saucepan over medium heat, melt the butter. When it's almost melted, whisk in the crème fraîche and cream, increase the heat to medium-high, and bring to a simmer. Whisk in the cheese, salt, and pepper and remove from the heat. Cover and set aside.

Reserve ½ cup of the pasta-cooking water, then drain the pasta and cauliflower. Return the pasta and cauliflower to the pot and stir in the Alfredo sauce and prosciutto, if using. Taste, ideally with your wine, and add more salt, pepper, and/or a little cooking water if you like. Serve hot, passing additional cheese at the table.

FOOD + WINE TIP If your Chardonnay is particularly crisp, have a few lemon wedges at the ready. A squeeze on top of the pasta will take the pairing from good to practically perfect.

crab salad sandwiches

This dish is inspired by a deliciously indulgent crab appetizer that my step-mom, Shannon, used to make. Turning it into a sandwich, brimming with even more crab, makes it even more so.

I especially recommend using lump crabmeat from a good fishmonger—it's sweeter and more succulent than canned crab, and there's nothing like biting into a nice big hunk of it. **Serves 4**

2 lemons
1 cup mayonnaise
1 shallot, minced
2 teaspoons prepared horseradish, or more to taste
1 teaspoon coarse kosher salt, or more to taste
1 pound cooked lump crabmeat, picked over
¼ cup chopped fresh flat-leaf parsley
4 soft sandwich rolls, split horizontally
1 large carrot, finely shredded (you should have about 1¼ cups)
3 cups loosely packed mixed salad greens (about 1½ ounces)

Finely grate the zest from the lemons. Halve the lemons and squeeze them to yield 2 tablespoons of juice (save the remaining lemons for another use). In a small bowl, combine the lemon zest, lemon juice, mayonnaise, shallot, horseradish, and salt. Set aside. (You can prepare the mayonnaise mixture up to 3 days in advance, storing it covered in the refrigerator.)

In a medium bowl, combine the crab and parsley. Add the mayonnaise mixture, gently tossing to combine. Taste, ideally with your wine, and add more lemon juice, horseradish, and/or salt if you like.

Arrange the crab mixture on the bottom halves of the rolls, dividing it evenly. Top with the carrot, the greens, and the top halves of the rolls and serve.

is it buttery or is it crisp?

Chardonnay can be crisp and bright, toasty and buttery—and everything in between. So when you're looking at a bottle in the wine shop, how can you tell which is which?

Sometimes there will be clues. If the label indicates that the wine is oak-aged, it will likely have toasty, oaky, and/or vanilla notes. If the label indicates stainless steel aging, the wine is likely more crisp. And if the label mentions malolactic or secondary fermentation, the wine will probably have buttery notes and less acidity.

That said, nothing takes the place of a knowledgeable retailer. If there's something in particular you're looking for—be it a style of Chardonnay or a pairing recommendation—just ask.

scallop scampi with peas and orzo

Another classic, deliciously indulgent combination of flavors that's ridiculously easy to make at home. If you like, you can substitute shrimp for the scallops, or use a combination of both. **Serves 4**

- 6 ounces orzo pasta
- 1 cup fresh or frozen peas, thawed if frozen
- 2 tablespoons all-purpose flour
- 1¼ pounds sea scallops (12 to 18) (see below)
- 2 tablespoons extra virgin olive oil
- 4 cloves garlic, smashed
- 4 tablespoons (½ stick) unsalted butter, divided
- ¼ cup Chardonnay, or other dry white wine
- 1½ teaspoons coarse kosher salt, or more to taste
- ½ teaspoon freshly ground black pepper, or more to taste
- 4 scallions, white and light green parts only, sliced
- 1 tablespoon fresh lemon juice

In a large pot of boiling, well-salted water (1 tablespoon of coarse kosher salt per quart), cook the pasta according to package directions. Stir in the peas, if fresh, 3 minutes before the pasta is al dente.

Meanwhile, place the flour in a small bowl. Lightly dredge the scallops in the flour. In a large skillet over medium-high heat, warm the olive oil. Add the scallops and cook until browned, about 1 minute per side. Add the peas, if previously frozen, garlic, and 2 tablespoons of the butter and cook, stirring occasionally, until the scallops are just cooked through, 1 to 2 minutes. Add the wine, salt, and pepper and cook, stirring, until the liquid comes to a boil. Remove the skillet from the heat and stir in the scallions, lemon juice, and remaining 2 tablespoons of butter. Taste, ideally with your wine, and add more salt and/or pepper if you like.

Drain the pasta, then transfer to a platter or plates. Top with the scallop mixture and serve hot.

NOTE Sea scallops are 1½ to 2 inches in diameter, as opposed to bay scallops, which are about ½ inch. Look for ones that have a slightly beige or pinkish hue. If they're stark white, it's a sign that they've been soaked in water—which increases their weight (meaning you're paying for water) and makes them less likely to get nicely browned.

grilled grouper with 'cress and 'cado relish

Crunchy, creamy, and with the slightest hint of heat—thanks to peppery watercress and spicy wasabi—this relish is a delicious accessory to the fish, and perfectly complements the wine.

To choose a sustainable fish, check with www.seafoodwatch.org for the latest on grouper. You can also substitute another firm, white, large-flake fish, such as sturgeon, halibut, or sea bass. • **Serves 4**

3 tablespoons white or golden balsamic vinegar (see note on page 23)
1 teaspoon soy sauce
½ teaspoon prepared wasabi paste (see below)
6 tablespoons mayonnaise, divided
2¼ teaspoons coarse kosher salt, divided, or more to taste
1 large avocado, pitted, peeled, and cut into ½-inch cubes
1 cup coarsely chopped watercress (about ½ ounce), plus 3 cups loosely packed watercress leaves (about 1½ ounces)
¼ cup ¼-inch diced peeled jicama
2 scallions, white and light green parts only, sliced on a diagonal
¾ teaspoon freshly ground black pepper
Four 6-ounce grouper fillets, ¾ to 1 inch thick, skin removed if you like
1½ teaspoons sesame seeds, toasted (see below)

▓ In a medium bowl, combine the vinegar, soy sauce, wasabi, 2 tablespoons of the mayonnaise, and ¾ teaspoon of the salt, whisking to dissolve the salt. Add the avocado, chopped watercress, jicama, and scallions, gently tossing to combine. Set aside.

▓ In a small bowl, combine the pepper, remaining ¼ cup of mayonnaise, and remaining 1½ teaspoons of salt. Set aside. (You can prepare the relish and the mayonnaise mixture up to an hour in advance, storing them covered in the refrigerator. Return the relish to room temperature before serving.)

▓ Prepare the grill to medium-high heat. Brush both sides of the fish with the mayonnaise mixture. Grill until cooked through, about 3 minutes per side.

▓ Arrange the watercress leaves on a platter or plates and place the fish on top. Top with the relish, sprinkle with the sesame seeds, and serve hot.

NOTES Wasabi is available in the Asian section of most major supermarkets. Besides using it in this recipe, you can use it in sushi and other Asian or Asian-inspired dishes, and in place of horseradish.

To toast seeds: In a small skillet over medium heat, stir the seeds until lightly browned and, depending on the seeds, fragrant. It should take 1 to 3 minutes, depending on the type of seed and the amount in the skillet. Transfer to a plate and set aside to cool.

potato-crusted alaskan halibut with garlic and tarragon

Shredded potatoes give sweet, succulent halibut fillets a hash-browns familiarity, but also a dressed-up crisp, crunchy coating.

To help the potatoes adhere to the fish, follow the directions carefully—make especially sure to thoroughly heat the skillets and the oil before adding the fish. And resist the temptation to soak the shredded potatoes in water—soaking can help avoid browning, but it can also rinse off the potatoes' helpfully sticky starches. • **Serves 6**

1½ pounds Yukon gold or russet potatoes
 Six 6-ounce Alaskan halibut fillets, ¾ to 1 inch thick, skin removed
2 teaspoons coarse kosher salt, divided
1 teaspoon freshly ground black pepper, divided
¼ cup extra virgin olive oil
6 cloves garlic, thinly sliced
4 tablespoons (½ stick) unsalted butter, divided
1 tablespoon chopped fresh tarragon

▓ Shred the potatoes (you should have at least 3 cups). Squeeze the liquid from the potatoes and set aside.

▓ Working quickly to prevent the potatoes from browning, use paper towels to pat the fish fillets dry, then arrange them on a work surface. Sprinkle one side of the fish with 1 teaspoon of the salt and ½ teaspoon of the pepper. Top each fillet with about ¼ cup of the shredded potatoes, spreading them evenly and patting them to adhere. Carefully overturn the fillets onto one or two plates. Sprinkle the other side of the fish with the remaining 1 teaspoon of salt and remaining ½ teaspoon of pepper. Top each fillet with ¼ cup of the shredded potatoes, spreading them evenly and patting them to adhere (you might not need all the potatoes).

▓ In each of 2 very large nonstick skillets over medium-high heat, warm 2 tablespoons of the olive oil. Carefully slide 3 fillets into each skillet. Cook until the potatoes are golden brown on the bottom, 3 or 4 minutes. Carefully turn and cook until the fish is cooked through and the potatoes are golden brown on the bottom, 2 to 3 minutes. Transfer the fish to a platter or plates. (If you don't have 2 very large nonstick skillets, cook the fish in batches.)

▓ Remove any stray potato shreds and return one of the skillets to medium-high heat (remove the other from the heat). Add the garlic and 1 tablespoon of the butter and cook, stirring, until tender, about 1 minute. Remove the skillet from the heat, add the remaining 3 tablespoons of butter, and stir until it melts. Stir in the chopped tarragon. Spoon the sauce over the halibut and serve hot.

grilled chicken with marinated peppers

You need to start a day or so ahead to marinate the peppers. But you'll be rewarded with a juicy, succulent mixture that, besides being pretty, wonderfully echoes the richness in the wine.

The whole setup is served on top of a piece of toasted sourdough bread—all the better to soak up every yummy drop. • **Serves 6**

    1 large red bell pepper
    1 large yellow or orange bell pepper
    1 large green bell pepper
    1 small orange
    3 tablespoons white or golden balsamic vinegar (see note on page 23)
    3 cloves garlic, thinly sliced
    9 tablespoons extra virgin olive oil, divided
    1 tablespoon coarse kosher salt, divided
 1½ teaspoons freshly ground black pepper, divided
    6 large boneless chicken breasts (2½ to 3 pounds), ideally skin-on
      Six ½-inch-thick slices crusty artisan sourdough bread

▥ Prepare the grill to medium-high heat. Place the bell peppers on the grill and cook, turning occasionally, until well charred, 12 to 18 minutes. (You can also char the peppers directly over a medium flame on a gas stovetop. Sit them each right on the grate over a burner and cook, turning occasionally, until charred all over, 8 to 12 minutes.) Cover and set aside until cool enough to handle.

▥ Meanwhile, use a vegetable peeler to cut the colored part of the peel from half of the orange. Cut the peel crosswise into thin slices (save the remaining orange for another use). Set aside.

▥ Wipe most of the charred skin from the peppers, then halve the peppers and discard the core and seeds. Cut the peppers into ¼-inch slices. In a medium bowl, combine the peppers, orange peel, vinegar, garlic, 6 tablespoons of the olive oil, 1 teaspoon of the salt, and ½ teaspoon of the black pepper. Transfer the mixture to a container, cover, and refrigerate for 1 to 3 days, stirring occasionally.

▥ Prepare the grill to medium-high heat. Brush both sides of the chicken and bread with the remaining 3 tablespoons of olive oil. Sprinkle the chicken with the remaining 2 teaspoons of salt and remaining 1 teaspoon of black pepper. Grill the chicken until it's cooked through, 3 to 4 minutes per side. During the last 2 minutes, place the bread on the grill and turn it to lightly toast both sides. Top each piece of toasted bread with a piece of chicken, transfer to a platter or plates, and let the chicken rest, loosely covered with foil, for 5 minutes.

▥ Top the chicken with the pepper mixture, dividing evenly, and serve.

classic roast chicken with roast potatoes

Chardonnay and roast chicken, in pretty much any form, is considered a classic pairing. Here, a lemon roasted inside the cavity gets squeezed over the final dish, giving it a brightness that takes the combination to new heights. **Serves 4 to 6**

> 1 cup reduced-sodium chicken broth
> 18 small red or white potatoes (about 1½ pounds), or a combination
> ¼ cup extra virgin olive oil, divided
> 1 tablespoon coarse kosher salt, divided
> 1½ teaspoons freshly ground black pepper, divided
> One 3½- to 4-pound chicken
> 1 tablespoon herbes de Provence (see below)
> 1 lemon, halved

▨ Preheat the oven to 425°F. Pour the broth into a 9 x 13-inch baking pan. Set aside.

▨ In a medium bowl, combine the potatoes, 2 tablespoons of the olive oil, 1 teaspoon of the salt, and ½ teaspoon of the pepper, tossing to coat the potatoes. Arrange the potatoes in a single layer in the baking pan. Set aside.

▨ Rub the chicken all over with the remaining 2 tablespoons of olive oil. Sprinkle the chicken inside and out with the herbes de Provence, remaining 2 teaspoons of salt, and remaining 1 teaspoon of pepper. Place the lemon halves inside the chicken (if both won't fit, place one in the pan with the potatoes). Tie the legs together and tuck in the wings. Set the chicken on the potatoes, breast side up. Roast for 30 minutes.

▨ Baste the chicken with the pan juices. Continue roasting, basting about every 15 minutes, until an internal thermometer inserted in the thickest part of the thigh reads 165°F and the potatoes are browned and tender, about 1¼ hours total cooking time. Let the chicken rest, loosely covered with foil, for 10 minutes before carving. (It will continue to cook, reaching an internal temperature of about 175°F.)

▨ Carve the chicken and arrange on a platter or plates with the potatoes on the side. Squeeze the lemon from the chicken cavity over the chicken and potatoes. Drizzle with any pan juices, if you like, and serve.

NOTE Herbes de Provence is a wonderful mixture of dried herbs that might include basil, rosemary, sage, marjoram, thyme, and, sometimes, lavender. Look for it in the spice section of most major supermarkets or at specialty food stores. It's sometimes packaged in a small clay crock. Besides using it in this recipe, you can sprinkle herbes de Provence on roasting pork and lamb and stir it into summer tomato pasta.

chicken with rice is nice stovetop casserole

This recipe was inspired by my friend and former coworker Kate, who was always moved to sing a little song from her childhood at the notion of chicken with rice, and also by my mom, whose best meals were tasty concoctions all cooked together in the same Le Creuset pot. **Serves 4**

    4 bone-in, skin-on chicken thighs (1¾ to 2¼ pounds)
 1½ teaspoons coarse kosher salt, or more to taste
    ½ teaspoon freshly ground black pepper, or more to taste
    1 tablespoon extra virgin olive oil
    2 cloves garlic, pressed through a garlic press or minced
 1¼ cups reduced-sodium chicken broth
    ⅓ cup Chardonnay, or other dry white wine
    1 large carrot, cut into ½-inch dice
    1 leek, white and light green parts only, cut into ½-inch slices
 12 small white or brown mushrooms, halved
    1 cup uncooked white and wild rice blend (see below)
    2 tablespoons chopped fresh thyme

▨ Sprinkle both sides of the chicken with the salt and pepper.

▨ In a large skillet over medium-high heat, warm the olive oil. Add the chicken, skin side down, and cook until brown, 3 to 4 minutes. Turn and brown the other side, 3 to 4 minutes. Transfer the chicken to a plate and set aside.

▨ Add the garlic and cook, stirring, for 10 seconds. Add the broth and wine (be careful—the mixture may splatter) and scrape up any browned bits on the bottom of the skillet. Stir in the carrot, leek, mushrooms, rice, and thyme. Nestle the chicken and any accumulated juices back into the skillet and bring to a boil. Reduce to a simmer, cover, and cook until the liquid is absorbed, the rice is tender, and the chicken is cooked through, about 25 minutes. Taste, ideally with your wine, and add salt and/or pepper if you like.

▨ Serve hot, with the chicken on top of the rice mixture.

> **NOTE** White and wild rice have different cooking times. But when a mixture contains both, the wild rice has been partially cooked so that it'll be ready at the same time as the white rice. In other words, be sure to use an already-mixed **white and wild rice blend**, or your white rice will be done when your wild rice is still very al dente.

FOOD + WINE TIP You might be tempted to drain the fat in the pan after browning the chicken. Resist the urge. That extra richness helps marry the dish to typically rich Chardonnay.

viognier

The first time I ever had Viognier was at my friend Catrine's house. Catrine grew up in France, around wine, and to me had head-to-toe vin-sophistication. She poured me a glass of this rich, beautifully aromatic white and it was love at first sip.

Since then, I've come to think of Viognier (vee-ohn-YAY) as the hothouse flower of wines. It's heady and inviting. It's exotic. It's lovely to enjoy. But sometimes it has to be handled carefully. By that I mean, while Viognier's richness helps it pair with many of the same dishes that work with Chardonnay, and its aromatic qualities add the opportunity for exotic ingredients, Viognier can also have a mineral-y, almost steely quality that can make pairings challenging. Just baby it—and you, too, might fall for Viognier.

viognier by another name

• **Condrieu.** This name comes from the area in France's Rhône Valley known for Viognier.

pairing with viognier

Although there are, of course, nuances to Viognier, the most important factors in food and wine pairing aren't a wine's nuances, but its broad strokes. If you learn a wine's overall characteristics and combine that information with the General Pairing Tips (page 8), you'll have a near-perfect pairing every time.

Broad characteristics:
• dry (not sweet)
• medium-low to medium in acidity, crispness, or brightness
• no or very low tannins
• medium to heavy weight
• medium to strong intensity

Pairs well with dishes that are:
• not sweet
• medium-low to medium in acidity, crispness, or brightness
• medium to heavy weight
• medium to strong intensity
(Because the wine has no or very low tannins, they're not a factor.)
For example, chicken curry, macadamia-crusted halibut, or roasted root vegetables.

fine-tuning

As with Chardonnay, you can almost never go wrong adding more richness to a dish you'll be pairing with Viognier. Try cream, butter, mayonnaise, soft cheeses, and even toasted nuts.

But a word of caution: Be careful with acidity or bitterness. Too much can wash out the fruit and accentuate a steely, austere quality that Viognier can sometimes have.

other nuances

Once you have a pairing that's working on the basis of sweetness, acidity, weight, and intensity, you can start playing with subtler nuances.

Some of the subtle flavors that you might find in a Viognier include stone fruits, pear, citrus, baking spices, floral notes, and minerality. So it works to add those flavors, or foods that complement them, to your dishes.

other thoughts

Some foods that are considered classic pairings with Viognier are creamy cheeses, chicken (especially roasted), richer fish and shellfish (especially crab and lobster), curries, toasted nuts, pork, and anything with butter, cream, or a buttery/creamy sauce.

butternut squash and goat cheese puff pastry tart

I do a lot of versions of this tart, varying the toppings depending on the season and the wine I'm planning to serve it with. Here, creamy butternut squash marries the dish to similarly rich Viognier—and just a touch of fresh ginger provides enough brightness to match up to the wine's sometimes-steely notes. ▪ **Serves 3 or 4**

- 3 tablespoons unsalted butter
- 1 pound butternut squash (about ½ medium), seeded, peeled, and cut into ½-inch dice (you should have about 2¼ cups) (see below)
- 1 teaspoon freshly grated ginger
- ¾ teaspoon coarse kosher salt, or more to taste
- ½ teaspoon freshly ground black pepper, or more to taste
- ¼ teaspoon ground allspice
- 1 sheet puff pastry (half of a 17.3-ounce package), thawed
- ½ cup chèvre (spreadable goat cheese) (about 4 ounces)
- 2 scallions, white and light green parts only, thinly sliced

▓ In a large skillet over medium heat, melt the butter. Add the squash and cook, stirring occasionally, until the squash is tender, 5 to 8 minutes. Add the ginger, salt, pepper, and allspice and cook, stirring, until the ginger is fragrant, about 30 seconds. Remove from the heat. Taste the squash mixture, ideally with your wine, and add more salt and/or pepper if you like. (You can prepare the squash mixture up to 2 days in advance, storing it covered in the refrigerator. Return it to room temperature before proceeding.)

▓ Line a baking sheet with parchment. On a lightly floured surface, roll out the puff pastry to a 10-inch square. Transfer to the prepared baking sheet. Using a fork, pierce the pastry all over. Place the baking sheet in the refrigerator for 20 minutes. (You can refrigerate the pastry, covered, for up to a day.)

▓ Preheat the oven to 400°F.

▓ Crumble about three-quarters of the cheese on the pastry, leaving a 1-inch border. Arrange the squash mixture on top, then crumble on the remaining cheese. Bake the tart until golden, about 25 minutes.

▓ Sprinkle the scallions over the tart, cut it into pieces, and serve hot.

NOTE The hardest thing about making this super-easy tart is tackling the squash. Use a sharp knife to cut it in half, use a large spoon to scrape out the seeds, then use a vegetable peeler to remove the peel. If the squash is proving difficult to halve, pierce it a few times, then microwave it for a couple of minutes, which will soften it up.

wine-y macaroni and jarlsberg cheese

Because of its wine-infused flavor and the slightly sophisticated taste of nutty Jarlsberg, you could also call this "Adult Macaroni and Cheese." It would be great at a casual dinner party. **Serves 6 to 8**

6 tablespoons (¾ stick) unsalted butter
6 shallots, cut into ¼-inch dice (you should have about 1 cup)
6 tablespoons all-purpose flour
2 cups milk (low-fat is okay)
1 cup Viognier, or other dry white wine
8 ounces Jarlsberg cheese, shredded (you should have about 2 cups)
½ cup crème fraîche
1 tablespoon coarse kosher salt
1½ teaspoons Dijon mustard
1 teaspoon ground nutmeg, preferably freshly grated
1 pound elbow macaroni pasta
⅓ cup grated Parmesan cheese (1½ to 2 ounces)
⅓ cup panko (Japanese-style breadcrumbs)
2 tablespoons extra virgin olive oil

▨ In a large saucepan over medium heat, melt the butter. Add the shallots and cook, stirring occasionally, until tender, 2 to 3 minutes. Sprinkle in the flour and, whisking constantly, cook for 2 minutes. Slowly add the milk, whisking out any lumps of flour. Add the wine and cook, stirring occasionally, until the sauce thickens and comes to a simmer, 4 to 5 minutes. Remove from the heat and stir in the Jarlsberg, crème fraîche, salt, mustard, and nutmeg. Set aside.

▨ In a large pot of boiling, well-salted water (1 tablespoon of coarse kosher salt per quart), cook the pasta according to package directions.

▨ Meanwhile, preheat the oven to 400°F. Oil a 2-quart casserole dish with safflower, sunflower, peanut, or other high-heat cooking oil. In a medium bowl, combine the Parmesan, panko, and olive oil. Set aside.

▨ Drain the pasta and return it to the pot. Stir in the cheese sauce. Transfer the entire mixture to the prepared casserole dish. Sprinkle the Parmesan mixture over the top. Place the casserole dish on a rimmed baking sheet and bake until the top is nicely browned, 20 to 25 minutes. Serve hot.

FOOD + WINE TIP Also great with Chardonnay.

macadamia-crusted sturgeon with brown butter papaya

I've been hearing a lot about brown butter recently—one magazine even dubbed it the flavor of the year! All of which might make you think it somehow fussy or challenging to make. But the truth is that brown butter is as simple as, well, browning butter. In other words, letting it cook until the milk solids in the butter turn golden brown, at which point they contribute deliciously nutty notes to whatever you're cooking—notes that classically pair with Viognier.

Although domestic sturgeon is a delicious, and sustainable, option, this dish would also be good with other firm, white-fleshed fishes, such as halibut, sea bass, or tilapia. • **Serves 4**

> Four 6-ounce sturgeon fillets, about 1 inch thick, skin removed if you like
> 1 large egg white, lightly beaten
> 1½ teaspoons coarse kosher salt, divided, or more to taste
> ½ cup chopped macadamia nuts
> 4 teaspoons canola, grapeseed, or other neutral-flavored oil
> 4 tablespoons (½ stick) unsalted butter, cut into 3 or 4 pieces
> 1 papaya, peeled, seeded, and cut into ¼-inch slices
> 2 tablespoons fresh lime juice (1 or 2 limes), or more to taste

▨ Preheat the oven to 350°F. Spray a rimmed baking sheet with nonstick cooking spray.

▨ Brush the top (the side that didn't have the skin) of the fish with the egg white (you might not need it all) and sprinkle with 1 teaspoon of the salt. Press the macadamia nuts evenly over that side of the fish.

▨ In a very large skillet over medium heat, warm the oil. Add the fish, crusted side down, and cook until the nuts are browned, about 2 minutes. Carefully transfer the fish to the prepared baking sheet, arranging it crusted side up. Bake until cooked through, about 10 minutes.

▨ Meanwhile, wipe out the skillet and return it to medium heat. Add the butter and let it melt, stirring occasionally, until it turns golden brown, about 2 minutes. Add the papaya and cook, stirring, until heated through. Remove from the heat and stir in the lime juice and remaining ½ teaspoon of salt. Taste, ideally with your wine, and add more salt and/or lime juice if you like. Set aside until the fish is done.

▨ Transfer the papaya mixture to a platter or plates. Arrange the fish on top, drizzle with any remaining juices in the skillet, and serve hot.

FOOD + WINE TIP A sweet food can make a dry wine taste sour—so if your papaya is particularly sweet, you might need extra lime juice to balance it out.

lobster tails with vanilla drawn butter

Here, a simple yet classic dish is given an exotic spin with an infusion of vanilla bean. The resulting rich, floral butter sauce is an ideal match for rich, floral Viognier. • **Serves 4**

1 vanilla bean
1 cup (2 sticks) unsalted butter, cut into 6 or 8 pieces
1¼ teaspoons coarse kosher salt, divided
Four 10- to 12-ounce lobster tails, thawed if frozen, cut lengthwise in half

▥ Use a small sharp knife to split the vanilla bean in half lengthwise. With the tip of the knife, scrape out the seeds and set them aside. Cut the remaining pod in half and place it in a small saucepan along with the butter. Place the saucepan over medium heat and melt the butter. Remove from the heat and set aside for 10 minutes.

▥ Use a shallow spoon to skim any foam off the top of the melted butter. As if you were decanting a wine with sediment at the bottom of the bottle, pour the melted butter into a small bowl, leaving the milk solids and vanilla pod behind. Discard the solids (you can rinse and save the pod for another use). Add the reserved vanilla seeds and ¾ teaspoon of the salt to the drawn butter, stirring to dissolve the salt. (You can prepare the vanilla butter in advance, storing it covered in the refrigerator for up to 3 days or in the freezer for several months. Thaw in the refrigerator, then gently remelt it before proceeding.)

▥ Prepare the grill to medium-low heat or preheat the broiler and arrange a rack about 6 inches from the heat. Set aside all but 2 table-spoons of the vanilla butter. Arrange the lobster, meat side up, on a rimmed baking sheet. Brush with the 2 tablespoons of vanilla butter and sprinkle with the remaining ½ teaspoon of salt. Grill or broil the lobster, meat side up, for 5 minutes. Turn the lobster and grill or broil until cooked through, about 3 minutes.

▥ Serve the lobster hot, with the reserved vanilla drawn butter on the side for dipping.

FOOD + WINE TIP As is the case with many of the recipes in this chapter, this dish would also pair well with Chardonnay.

buttermilk oven-fried chicken with garlicky ranch sauce

If you like the idea of crispy, crunchy chicken, but don't like the idea of frying, this recipe is for you. The coating cooks up finger-lickin' good, and the meat stays deliciously moist, thanks to an up-to-overnight buttermilk marinade. • **Serves 4 to 6**

⅔ cup sour cream
2 tablespoons extra virgin olive oil
1½ teaspoons granulated garlic powder
1½ teaspoons honey
1 teaspoon finely chopped fresh dill
½ teaspoon Dijon mustard
½ teaspoon granulated onion powder
¼ teaspoon white pepper, ideally freshly ground
3¼ cups buttermilk, divided
¼ cup plus 1 teaspoon coarse kosher salt, divided
2 tablespoons freshly ground black pepper, divided
One 3½- to 4-pound chicken, cut into 8 pieces
2 cups all-purpose flour
1 tablespoon paprika

▓ In a medium bowl, combine the sour cream, olive oil, garlic powder, honey, dill, mustard, onion powder, white pepper, ¼ cup of the buttermilk, and 1 teaspoon of the salt, whisking to dissolve the salt. Cover and set aside in the refrigerator for 8 hours to allow the flavors to bloom. (You can prepare the sauce up to 1 week in advance, storing it covered in the refrigerator.)

▓ In another medium bowl, combine the remaining 3 cups of buttermilk, 2 tablespoons of the remaining salt, and 1 tablespoon of the black pepper, whisking to dissolve the salt. Place the chicken in a large resealable bag, add the buttermilk mixture, and seal, squeezing out as much air as possible. Set aside in the refrigerator for 4 to 24 hours, turning occasionally.

▓ Preheat the oven to 400°F. Oil a rimmed baking sheet with safflower, sunflower, peanut, or other high-heat cooking oil.

▓ In a large shallow bowl, combine the flour, paprika, remaining 2 tablespoons of salt, and remaining 1 tablespoon of black pepper. One piece at a time, remove the chicken from the marinade, shaking off the excess, then dip it in the flour mixture, shaking off the excess (discard the marinade). Set the coated chicken on the prepared baking sheet and bake until the chicken is nicely browned and cooked through, about 45 minutes.

▓ Serve the chicken hot or at room temperature, with the garlicky ranch sauce on the side.

curried chicken and avocado salad

This is a version of the classic chicken salad in an avocado boat—except that the "boat" is sliced. To round out the meal, add a cup of crab bisque, a sourdough roll, and butter. • **Serves 6**

> 1 cup mayonnaise
> ¼ cup fresh lemon juice (about 2 lemons), or more to taste
> 2 teaspoons coarse kosher salt, or more to taste
> 1½ teaspoons curry powder
> 1 teaspoon freshly ground black pepper, or more to taste
> 2 large cooked boneless, skinless chicken breasts, cut into ½-inch dice (you should have about 4 cups)
> ½ cup chopped celery
> ½ cup chopped red onion
> ¼ cup coarsely chopped fresh flat-leaf parsley, plus sprigs for garnish
> 1 head butter lettuce, separated into leaves
> 3 avocados, peeled, pitted, and thinly sliced

▒ In a medium bowl, combine the mayonnaise, lemon juice, salt, curry powder, and pepper. Set aside. (You can prepare the mayonnaise mixture up to 3 days in advance, storing it covered in the refrigerator.)

▒ In a large bowl, combine the chicken, celery, onion, and chopped parsley. Add about ⅔ cup of the mayonnaise mixture, gently tossing to combine. Taste, ideally with your wine, and add more lemon juice, salt, and/or pepper if you like.

▒ Arrange the lettuce leaves on plates and fan the avocado slices on top. Drizzle the remaining mayonnaise mixture over the lettuce and avocado. Mound the chicken mixture in the center of the plates, dividing it evenly. Garnish with the parsley sprigs and serve.

avoid this rookie mistake

It's completely logical to think that since there are fruit flavors in wine, adding similar fruits to food will help a pairing—for example, adding oranges to a chicken dish to help it pair with a citrusy Viognier. The reality, however, is that since most fruit is sweet, adding fruit to a food will usually make a wine pairing worse—the wine will taste more acidic and/or more bitter, per Fine-Tuning Tip 2 (page 9).

So instead, try adding fruit flavors without adding fruit per se—for example, using orange zest. You can also try dried fruits, which tend to be less sweet than their fresh counterparts. Or try tart fruits, like raspberries.

If none of those tricks is working and your wine is tasting sour or bitter, chalk it up as a rookie mistake and switch to an off-dry, or slightly sweet, wine.

pork medallions with orange hollandaise and hazelnuts

Traditionally, hollandaise is made with lemon juice and sometimes a dab of Dijon mustard. Here, we're omitting the mustard and adding orange zest and juice. It gives the familiar sauce a bit of the unexpected—and beautifully complements the fruity, floral qualities in the wine.

On the side, try roasted carrots, rice, or steamed cauliflower.

Serves 6

1 orange
3 large egg yolks
1 tablespoon fresh lemon juice
About ¾ cup (1½ sticks) unsalted butter, melted, divided
⅛ teaspoon white pepper, ideally freshly ground
1¼ teaspoons coarse kosher salt, divided
Two 1-pound pork tenderloins, trimmed, ideally brined (see page 81), and cut diagonally into ½-inch slices
½ cup chopped hazelnuts, toasted (see note on page 18)

Finely grate the zest from the orange (you should have about 1½ teaspoons packed). Halve the orange and squeeze it to yield 2 tablespoons of juice (save any remaining orange for another use). Set the zest and juice aside.

In the bottom of a double boiler or in a medium saucepan, bring 1 inch of water to a boil over high heat. Reduce to a simmer. In the top of the double boiler or in a medium bowl set over the saucepan without touching the water, combine the orange zest, orange juice, yolks, and lemon juice. In a slow, steady stream, whisk in ½ cup of the butter. Continue to whisk until the sauce reaches 140°F. Maintain this temperature and cook, adjusting the heat and/or moving the top of the double boiler off the bottom as necessary and whisking constantly, for 3 minutes. Remove from the heat and stir in the pepper and ¼ teaspoon of the salt. Cover to keep warm and set aside.

In a very large skillet over medium heat, warm 2 tablespoons of the remaining butter. Sprinkle the pork with the remaining 1 teaspoon of salt. Add half of the pork to the skillet and cook until browned and cooked through, 2 to 4 minutes per side. Transfer the cooked pork to a platter or plates, cover to keep warm, and repeat with the remaining pork, adding more melted butter as needed.

Arrange the pork on a platter or plates. Drizzle the hollandaise sauce on top, sprinkle with the hazelnuts, and serve hot.

riesling

The first time that the food and wine pairing lightbulb went off in my head, when I had a combination that really underscored how good a good combination could be, it was thanks to a bottle of Riesling. My now-husband and I were at a restaurant in San Francisco and it was one of those perfect evenings—the atmosphere, the service, the food, the company. But what sticks in my mind is the smoked sea bass, the Riesling, and thinking, "Oh. My. God."

That was about fifteen years ago, and Riesling (REES-ling) is still one of my favorites. It's fruity, light, and refreshing. It's great for sipping—and great for pairing with food.

riesling by another name

• White Riesling, Johannisberg Riesling. There are a lot of wines and grape names with the word *Riesling* in them—but these two, along with Riesling Renano, are the only ones made from the true Riesling grape. Johannisberg Riesling was once a popular name for California Rieslings, but it's not used anymore.

pairing with riesling

Although there are, of course, nuances to Riesling, the most important factors in food and wine pairing aren't a wine's nuances, but its broad strokes. If you learn a wine's overall characteristics and combine that information with the General Pairing Tips (page 8), you'll have a near-perfect pairing every time.

Broad characteristics:
• dry to off-dry (very slightly sweet)
• medium to high in acidity, crispness, or brightness
• no or very low tannins
• light to medium weight
• light to medium intensity
(The wine is available much sweeter, but because we're dealing with savory recipes, we're limiting the discussion to dry and off-dry.)

Pairs well with dishes that are:
• not sweet to very slightly sweet
• medium to high in acidity, crispness, or brightness
• light to medium weight
• light to medium intensity
(Because the wine has no or very low tannins, they're not a factor.)

For example, honey-baked ham, fish with salsa verde, or sweet-and-sour chicken.

fine-tuning

Because Riesling can sometimes have a little sweetness, you can afford a little sweetness in the food—but only that. If either you have a dry Riesling or you end up with too much sweetness in the food and the wine is tasting sour, per Fine-Tuning Tip 1 (page 9), add acid and/or salt to the food. The acids that seem to best complement Riesling are ones that are similarly light and fruity—try lemon and lime juice, white or golden balsamic vinegar, and rice vinegar.

In addition to food that's a little sweet, an off-dry Riesling can taste great with food that's a little spicy.

other nuances

Once you have a pairing that's working on the basis of sweetness, acidity, weight, and intensity, you can start playing with subtler nuances.

Some of the subtle flavors that you might find in a Riesling include stone fruits, apple, pear, tropical fruits, citrus, honey, floral notes, smoke, and steely and even petrol-like notes. So it works to add those flavors, or foods that complement them, to your dishes.

other thoughts

Some foods that are considered classic pairings with Riesling are Asian food (especially Thai food), pork and ham, poultry (even gamier types like goose and duck), fish and shellfish, smoked fish, and moderately spicy dishes.

not-so-sweet and sour veggie stir-fry with rice noodles

A typical sweet-and-sour dish can have a lot of sweetness, which can make food and wine pairing challenging. Here, the sweetness is only mild—plus it's balanced by good acidity, or sourness, in the form of vinegar. In total, the dish is perfect for a wine that also has a touch of sweetness and good acidity. A wine like Riesling.

A wine labeled "dry Riesling" will lack that touch of sweetness. While that style is okay here, a nondry Riesling is ideal. • **Serves 4**

   6 ounces rice noodles (see below)
   ¼ cup rice vinegar
   4 teaspoons cornstarch
   ¾ cup unsweetened pineapple juice
   2 tablespoons soy sauce
   3 tablespoons honey
   2 teaspoons sesame oil
   2 tablespoons safflower, sunflower, peanut, or other high-heat cooking oil
   1 large red bell pepper, cored, seeded, and cut into ¾-inch dice
   1 large green bell pepper, cored, seeded, and cut into ¾-inch dice
   1 red onion, cut into ¾-inch dice
   ¾ cup ½-inch diced fresh pineapple (about ¼ pineapple)
   1 cup shelled edamame beans, thawed if frozen
   ⅓ cup finely shredded red cabbage

▓ In a large pot of boiling, well-salted water (1 tablespoon of coarse kosher salt per quart), cook the noodles according to package directions. Drain and set aside.

▓ While the noodles are cooking, in a small bowl, combine the vinegar and cornstarch, whisking to dissolve the cornstarch. Whisk in the pineapple juice, soy sauce, honey, and sesame oil. Set aside.

▓ In a large wok or skillet over high heat, heat the oil. Add the bell peppers and cook, stirring, for 2 minutes. Add the onion and cook, stirring, until the vegetables are crisp-tender, about 2 minutes. Add the fresh pineapple, edamame, and juice mixture and cook, stirring occasionally, until the pineapple is heated through and the sauce comes to a boil and thickens, 1 to 2 minutes.

▓ Arrange the noodles on a platter or plates and top with the stir-fry mixture, dividing it evenly. Sprinkle with the cabbage and serve hot.

NOTE Rice noodles, the same noodles used to make pad thai, are available in the ethnic or Asian section of most major supermarkets. They usually come thin or thick, and either can be used here. If you can't find rice noodles, you can buy a boxed pad thai kit and use its noodles (discarding the sauce mix). Besides using them in this recipe, you can use rice noodles with other stir-fry dishes, in soups, and in cold noodle salads.

grilled teriyaki tofu and scallions

Here's a vegetarian dish that even omnivores will enjoy. Pressing, marinating (plan for two to four hours), and grilling the tofu "steaks" gives them a juicy, toothsome, and, well, meaty taste and texture.

On the side, try jasmine rice or a green salad tossed with an Asian-style dressing. ▪ **Serves 4**

> Two 14- to 16-ounce packages extra-firm tofu, drained
> ¾ cup aji-mirin sweet cooking rice seasoning (Japanese cooking wine) (see below)
> ½ cup soy sauce
> 1 tablespoon sesame oil
> ½ teaspoon dried crushed red pepper flakes
> ½ cup honey
> 12 scallions, root ends intact, trimmed to 8 inches long

▦ Cut each piece of tofu in half horizontally, making a total of four thick slabs. Cut each slab in half diagonally, making 8 triangles. Arrange a few layers of paper towels in a baking dish or rimmed baking sheet large enough to hold the tofu in a single layer, place the tofu on top, then place a few more layers of paper towels on top of the tofu. Place another baking dish or rimmed baking sheet on top, weigh the top with a few heavy cans or jars, and set aside at room temperature for 30 minutes or covered (the entire setup) in the refrigerator for up to a day.

▦ In a medium bowl, whisk together the aji-mirin, soy sauce, sesame oil, and red pepper flakes. Place the tofu in a large resealable bag, add the aji-mirin mixture, and seal, squeezing out as much air as possible. Set aside in the refrigerator for 2 to 4 hours, turning occasionally.

▦ Remove the tofu from the marinade and pat it dry. Combine ¼ cup of the marinade with the honey (discard the remaining marinade or save it for another use).

▦ Prepare the grill to medium heat and lightly oil the grill. Grill the tofu until lightly browned, 3 to 4 minutes per side. Brush both sides of the tofu with the honey mixture and cook until well browned, about 1 minute per side. Brush the scallions with the sauce and grill until limp and lightly charred, 1 to 2 minutes per side.

▦ Serve the tofu hot, with the scallions on top and the remaining honey sauce on the side.

NOTE Aji-mirin is available in the ethnic or Asian section of most major supermarkets. Besides using it in this recipe, you can use it in Hoisin Pork Tenderloin with Asian Salad (page 78), Cashew Chicken Stir-Fry (page 88), Sticky Asian Barbecued Baby Back Ribs (page 97), and in sauces, dressings, and other Asian or Asian-inspired dishes.

mahi mahi with mango salsa

This recipe is inspired by a recent trip to Hawaii, where it's ever-present on restaurant menus. Perhaps not surprisingly given all the delicious tropical fruits that Hawaiian chefs use to complement seafood, poultry, and even meats, Riesling has a major presence on many restaurant wine lists. Its fruity, refreshing, and sometimes-sweet qualities make it a perfect match for the fruity, refreshing, and sometimes-sweet cuisine.

If you have leftover salsa, serve it with chicken, fish, pork, or even tortilla chips. The resulting dish will—you guessed it—pair well with Riesling. • **Serves 6**

- 1 mango, peeled, pitted, and cut into ¼-inch dice (you should have about 1½ cups)
- ¼ red bell pepper, cored, seeded, and cut into ¼-inch dice
- ¼ small red onion, finely diced
- 2 scallions, white and light green parts only, thinly sliced
- ½ jalapeño, cored, seeded, and finely diced, or more to taste
- 3 tablespoons fresh lime juice (about 2 limes), or more to taste
- 2 tablespoons coarsely chopped fresh cilantro, plus sprigs for garnish
- 2 teaspoons coarse kosher salt, divided, or more to taste
  Six 6-ounce mahi mahi fillets, about 1 inch thick, skin removed
- 4½ teaspoons canola, grapeseed, or other neutral-flavored oil, or more for pan-searing
- 1 teaspoon freshly ground black pepper

▦ In a medium bowl, combine the mango, bell pepper, onion, scallions, jalapeño, lime juice, chopped cilantro, and ½ teaspoon of the salt. Taste, ideally with your wine, and add more jalapeño, lime juice, and/or salt if you like. (You can prepare the salsa up to 2 hours in advance, storing it covered in the refrigerator.)

▦ Prepare the grill to medium-high heat. Brush both sides of the fish with the oil and sprinkle with the black pepper and remaining 1½ teaspoons of salt. Grill until cooked through, about 3½ minutes per side.

▦ (You can also pan-sear the fish. In each of 2 medium skillets over medium-high heat, warm 1 tablespoon of the oil. Add the fish and cook until cooked through, about 3½ minutes per side.)

▦ Arrange the fish on a platter or plates. Top with the salsa, garnish with the cilantro sprigs, and serve hot.

FOOD + WINE TIP If your mango is particularly sweet, you might notice that the dish makes your wine taste a little sour. To fix this, add more lime juice to the salsa, a little at a time, until the dish and the wine nicely complement each other. Or serve the dish with wedges of lime on the side and let your guests make their own adjustments.

seafood and andouille jambalaya

Jambalaya might sound exotic—and it does have deliciously haunting flavors—but it's basically a simple, one-pot meal that, after a little chopping and cutting, comes together quickly and cleans up even more so.

Including a spicy sausage like andouille is pretty traditional, while additional proteins might include chicken, pork, ham, and/or seafood. In this version, seafood helps keep the dish a little lighter, which helps marry it to Riesling. • **Serves 6 to 8**

2 tablespoons (¼ stick) unsalted butter
2 tablespoons extra virgin olive oil
9 to 12 ounces cooked andouille sausage, halved lengthwise and cut diagonally into ½-inch slices
2 stalks celery, cut into ¼-inch dice
1 red bell pepper, cored, seeded, and cut into ¼-inch dice
1 green bell pepper, cored, seeded, and cut into ¼-inch dice
1 onion, cut into ¼-inch dice
4 cloves garlic, pressed through a garlic press or minced
2½ cups reduced-sodium chicken broth
One 14.5-ounce can diced tomatoes
3 tablespoons chopped fresh thyme
4½ teaspoons smoked paprika (see below)
1½ teaspoons coarse kosher salt
¼ teaspoon cayenne pepper
1½ cups white long-grain rice
12 ounces large, raw, peeled shrimp, preferably tail on
12 ounces bay scallops or sea scallops, halved or quartered if very large (see note on page 48)

▥ In a medium stockpot over medium heat, warm the butter and olive oil. Add the sausage and cook, stirring occasionally, until it begins to brown, about 3 minutes. Add the celery and bell peppers and cook, stirring occasionally, for 2 minutes. Add the onion and cook, stirring occasionally, for 5 minutes. Add the garlic and cook, stirring occasionally, until the vegetables are tender, about 1 minute.

▥ Stir in the broth, tomatoes (with their juices), thyme, paprika, salt, and cayenne, scraping up any browned bits on the bottom of the pot. Stir in the rice, bring to a boil, and reduce to a simmer. Cover and cook until the rice is almost tender, about 20 minutes. Stir in the shrimp and scallops, cover, and cook until the seafood is cooked through and the liquid is almost all absorbed, about 4 minutes. Serve hot.

NOTE Smoked paprika is available in the spice section of most major supermarkets and at specialty food stores. Besides using it in this recipe, you can use it in Roast Salmon and Potatoes with Romesco Sauce (page 108), Tilapia with Gazpacho Salsa (page 110), Steak Soft Tacos with Cilantro Slaw and Chipotle Cream (page 113), Cumin and Smoked Paprika Leg of Lamb (page 126), Spice-Rubbed Pork Chops with Grilled Tomato Sauce (page 155), and Smoky Lentil and Vegetable Stew (page 160). It's also great in rubs and stirred into salsa, soups, stews, and sauces.

cilantro-lime salmon over jasmine rice

This is one of the first dishes I ever made for my now-husband, one that helped win his heart. It has bright, bold flavors, but also richness from the fish and a delicacy from the soft cilantro. And the almost chartreuse sauce is beautiful next to the pink salmon and white rice.

Serves 4

2	cups loosely packed fresh cilantro leaves and tender stems, plus sprigs for garnish
	One 4-inch piece fresh ginger, peeled and cut into 5 or 6 pieces
6	tablespoons fresh lime juice (about 4 limes), or more to taste
6	cloves garlic
1½	teaspoons coarse kosher salt, or more to taste
1	teaspoon ground turmeric
½	teaspoon ground cumin
¾	cup extra virgin olive oil
1	cup jasmine rice
1¼	pounds salmon fillets, skin removed, cut into 1½-inch pieces

▒ In the bowl of a food processor, combine the cilantro leaves and stems, ginger, lime juice, garlic, salt, turmeric, cumin, and ¼ cup water and pulse to finely chop, scraping down the bowl as necessary. With the motor running, slowly add the olive oil and process until smooth, scraping down the bowl as necessary. Taste, ideally with your wine, and add more lime juice and/or salt if you like. (You can prepare the cilantro-lime sauce in advance, storing it covered in the refrigerator for up to 3 days or in the freezer for several months. Thaw in the refrigerator before proceeding.)

▒ In a medium saucepan, cook the rice according to package directions.

▒ About 5 minutes before the rice is done, in a skillet just large enough to hold the salmon in a single layer, over medium heat, bring the cilantro-lime sauce to a boil. Add the salmon and return to a boil. Reduce to a simmer, cover, and cook until the salmon is cooked through, 6 to 7 minutes.

▒ Transfer the rice to a platter or plates. Arrange the salmon on top, dividing it evenly. Spoon the sauce over the salmon, garnish with the cilantro sprigs, and serve hot.

FOOD + WINE TIP While this dish is great with Riesling, its weight—from the succulent salmon and the rich sauce—helps it work with richer Gewürztraminer as well.

vietnamese chicken sandwiches

Like Asian summer rolls, these sandwiches are packed with sweet, spicy, salty, and savory flavors. But here the fillings are piled onto a baguette, reflecting the French influence on Vietnamese cuisine.

If you don't have already-cooked chicken on hand, use the meat from about half of a supermarket rotisserie chicken. **Serves 4**

- 1 tablespoon rice vinegar
- ¼ teaspoon coarse kosher salt
- 2 tablespoons plus ¼ teaspoon sugar, divided
- 1½ cups finely shredded green cabbage or slaw mix (about 2 ounces)
- ¼ cup shredded carrot
- ¼ cup thinly sliced red onion
- 2 cloves garlic, smashed
- 2 teaspoons chili sauce, such as Sriracha (see below)
- 3 tablespoons fresh lime juice (about 2 limes)
- 1 tablespoon fish sauce (see below)
- 8 ounces cooked boneless, skinless chicken, shredded (you should have about 2¼ cups)
- 1 baguette, ideally a soft one
- 3 tablespoons mayonnaise
- ½ small cucumber, peeled, halved lengthwise, seeded, and thinly sliced
- 16 fresh cilantro sprigs

▧ In a large bowl, combine the vinegar, salt, and ¼ teaspoon of the sugar, whisking to dissolve the salt and sugar. Add the cabbage, carrot, and onion, tossing to combine. Set the mixture aside, stirring occasionally, for 30 minutes.

▧ Meanwhile, in a mortar and pestle, combine the garlic, chili sauce, and remaining 2 tablespoons of sugar and mash them to a paste. (If you don't have a mortar and pestle, combine them in a small bowl and mash to a coarse paste with the back of a spoon.) Add the lime juice and fish sauce, stirring to combine. In a medium bowl, combine the lime juice mixture and the chicken. (You can prepare the cabbage mixture and the chicken mixture up to 4 hours in advance, storing them covered in the refrigerator.)

▧ Trim the ends off the baguette and cut it crosswise into 4 lengths. Cut each length horizontally, so it'll open like a book. Gently fold each piece open and spread with the mayonnaise, dividing it evenly. Top with the chicken mixture, cucumber, cabbage mixture, and cilantro, dividing them evenly, and serve.

NOTE Sriracha and fish sauce are available in the ethnic or Asian section of most major supermarkets. Besides using them in this recipe, you can use them in other dressings and sauces and other Asian or Asian-inspired dishes. You can also use Sriracha any time you want to add heat to your cooking.

coriander and fennel seed cornish hens with cucumber sauce

This super-quick and easy dish is also good with salmon fillets instead of Cornish hens—cut the roasting time to about eight minutes—and goes just as well with Riesling.

Jasmine rice or steamed parsleyed potatoes would be great alongside. • **Serves 6**

  5 teaspoons fennel seeds
  5 teaspoons coriander seeds
2¾ teaspoons coarse kosher salt, divided
  1 teaspoon freshly ground black pepper, divided
  ½ cucumber, peeled, halved lengthwise, seeded, and cut into 3 or 4 pieces
  ½ cup plain yogurt (low-fat is okay)
  2 tablespoons sour cream
  6 fresh cilantro sprigs
  6 fresh dill sprigs
  2 cloves garlic
    Three 1¼- to 1½-pound Cornish hens, halved lengthwise
    Optional special equipment: electric spice or coffee grinder

▦ In an electric spice or coffee grinder, combine the fennel and coriander seeds and pulse to coarsely grind. (If you don't have an electric spice or coffee grinder, use a mortar and pestle to crush the seeds or place them in a small bowl and crush them with the end of a wooden spoon.) Stir in 2 teaspoons of the salt and ½ teaspoon of the pepper. Set aside. (You can prepare the spice mixture up to a week in advance, storing it in an airtight container at room temperature.)

▦ In the bowl of a food processor, combine the cucumber, yogurt, sour cream, cilantro, dill, garlic, remaining ¾ teaspoon of salt, and remaining ½ teaspoon of pepper and process to puree, scraping down the bowl as necessary. (You can prepare the cucumber sauce up to 4 hours in advance, storing it covered in the refrigerator.)

▦ Preheat the oven to 450°F. Oil a rimmed baking sheet with safflower, sunflower, peanut, or other high-heat cooking oil.

▦ Arrange the hens, skin side up, on the prepared baking sheet. Sprinkle with the spice mixture and roast until cooked through, 30 to 35 minutes. Let the hens rest, loosely covered with foil, for 10 minutes.

▦ Serve the hens hot, with the cucumber sauce on the side.

FOOD + WINE TIP This dish has just a touch of sweetness from the cucumber and from the sweet-evoking fennel, coriander, and herbs. So an off-dry Riesling is ideal. If you don't know if your Riesling is dry or off-dry, don't worry about it.

ginger-soy roast turkey breast

My dad makes the best grilled turkey. He starts with a whole turkey, stuffs tons of ginger and garlic under the skin, slathers the bird with soy sauce, then cooks the whole thing in a kettle-style grill, basting along the way. It's not exactly Thanksgiving-y, but it's killer good— a fabulous change of pace from the usual roast turkey and a great excuse to enjoy turkey other times of year.

This recipe is inspired by Dad's. It has similar flavors—but it uses a half breast and the oven, making the dish a little easier but no less tasty. • **Serves 4**

1 tablespoon safflower, sunflower, peanut, or other high-heat cooking oil, plus more for the baking sheet

5 tablespoons soy sauce, divided

One 2½- to 3-pound bone-in turkey breast half, ideally brined (see page 81)

2 cloves garlic, thinly sliced

One 2-inch piece fresh ginger, peeled and very thinly sliced on a diagonal, divided

½ cup reduced-sodium chicken broth

½ cup Riesling, or other dry or off-dry white wine

1 tablespoon cornstarch dissolved in 2 tablespoons cold water

▓ Preheat the oven to 400°F. Oil a rimmed baking sheet with safflower, sunflower, peanut, or other high-heat cooking oil.

▓ In a small bowl, combine the oil and 3 tablespoons of the soy sauce. Divide the mixture in half and set both halves aside.

▓ Place the turkey on the prepared baking sheet. Gently slip your fingers under the skin and slide in the garlic and about three-quarters of the ginger, distributing them evenly over the meat. Rub one-half of the soy sauce mixture evenly over both sides of the turkey. Roast, basting with the other half of the soy sauce mixture and/or pan juices every 15 or 20 minutes, until an internal thermometer inserted into the thickest part of the turkey reads 170°F, about 1 hour. Transfer the turkey to a cutting board and let it rest, loosely covered with foil, for 10 minutes. (It will continue to cook, reaching an internal temperature of about 180°F.)

▓ Meanwhile, in a small saucepan over medium heat, combine the broth, wine, remaining 2 tablespoons of soy sauce, and remaining one quarter of the ginger and bring to a boil. Stir in the cornstarch mixture and cook, stirring, until the sauce comes to a boil and thickens, 60 to 90 seconds. Strain out the ginger if you like, cover the sauce to keep it warm, and set aside.

▓ Carve the whole piece of breast meat off the bones, then slice it crosswise. Serve the turkey hot, drizzled with the sauce and any accumulated juices (or pass the sauce at the table).

hoisin pork tenderloin with asian salad

Here's another recipe that's quick and easy enough for a weeknight, yet interesting and gourmet enough for company. It's really pretty on the plate, too, with pink meat beautifully complemented by a small pile of colorful green, orange, and purple salad.

If by some miracle you have leftovers, pile them onto a roll for a crunchy, flavorful sandwich. **Serves 6**

   2 tablespoons rice vinegar
   1 tablespoon aji-mirin sweet cooking rice seasoning (Japanese cooking wine) (see note on page 70)
   1 tablespoon packed light brown sugar
   1 tablespoon sesame oil
   ½ teaspoon Chinese five-spice powder (see note on page 98)
   1 tablespoon plus 2 teaspoons soy sauce, divided
   ⅓ cup hoisin sauce (see below)
     Two 1-pound pork tenderloins, trimmed and ideally brined (see page 81)
   2 cups broccoli slaw (see below)
   1 carrot, shredded
   6 scallions, white and light green parts only, thinly sliced

▓ In a small bowl, combine the vinegar, aji-mirin, brown sugar, sesame oil, Chinese five-spice powder, and 2 teaspoons of the soy sauce, whisking to dissolve the sugar. Set aside. (You can prepare the dressing up to 3 days in advance, storing it covered in the refrigerator.)

▓ Preheat the oven to 450°F.

▓ In another small bowl, combine the hoisin sauce and remaining 1 tablespoon of soy sauce. Spread the mixture all over the pork. Place the pork on a rack in a 9 x 13-inch baking pan and pour any remaining hoisin mixture over the top. Add about ¼ inch of water to the bottom of the pan. Roast the pork until an internal thermometer reads 140°F for medium rare, 25 to 30 minutes. Transfer the pork to a cutting board and let it rest, loosely covered with foil, for 10 minutes. (It will continue to cook, reaching an internal temperature of about 150°F.)

▓ Meanwhile, in a medium bowl, combine the broccoli slaw, carrot, scallions, and dressing.

▓ Slice the pork on an angle. Serve the meat hot, drizzled with any accumulated juices, with the salad on the side.

NOTES **Hoisin sauce** is available in the ethnic or Asian section of most major supermarkets. Besides using it in this recipe, you can use it in stir-fry and dipping sauces, and in other Asian or Asian-inspired dishes. **Broccoli slaw**, usually a mixture of julienned broccoli stems, carrots, and red cabbage, is available with other prepackaged produce in the produce section of most major supermarkets.

brined pork loin chops with apples, shallots, and star anise

Star anise gives this otherwise simple dish a subtle, warm, exotically spicy quality—not spicy like chiles, but spicy like baking spices—and nicely complements the other ingredients in the dish.

If you're pressed for time, you can forgo the brining, but it does make for tastier, juicier meat (see next page for more about brining).

Serves 4

    4 boneless pork loin chops, about 1 inch thick
   10 whole star anise, divided
    1 tablespoon canola, grapeseed, or other neutral-flavored oil
    1 small tart apple, such as Granny Smith or Pippin, cored and cut into
      ¼-inch slices
    4 shallots, quartered lengthwise
   ⅓ cup apple juice
    2 tablespoons apple cider vinegar, or more to taste
    1 teaspoon soy sauce
    2 tablespoons (¼ stick) unsalted butter
   ½ teaspoon coarse kosher salt, or more to taste
   ¼ teaspoon freshly ground black pepper, or more to taste

▥ Brine the pork chops as directed on next page, adding 6 of the whole star anise to the brine.

▥ In a large skillet over medium-high heat, warm the oil. Add the pork chops and cook until browned on both sides, about 4 minutes per side. Transfer the chops to a plate and set aside.

▥ Return the skillet to medium heat and add the apple and shallots. Cook, stirring occasionally, for 1 minute. Add the apple juice, vinegar, soy sauce, and remaining 4 star anise and scrape up any browned bits on the bottom of the skillet. Return the pork to the skillet, nestling it in the liquid, and reduce to a simmer. Cover and cook until the pork is just cooked through, about 4 minutes.

▥ Transfer the pork to a platter or plates. Remove the skillet from the heat and stir in the butter, salt, and pepper. Taste the apple-shallot mixture, ideally with your wine, and add more vinegar, salt, and/or pepper to taste. Spoon the mixture over the pork and serve hot.

FOOD + WINE TIP If your Riesling is dry, as opposed to off-dry, or very slightly sweet, you may notice that the sweetness of the apple makes the wine taste a touch sour. Add a little more vinegar and/or salt to the apple-shallot mixture and the pairing should come right into balance.

how to brine

Brining makes a huge difference with relatively lean cuts of meat that can have a tendency to dry out, helping to keep the meat both juicy and flavorful. If you have the time, I highly recommend it, particularly for pork. It's also great for turkey, especially for a whole bird, because it helps prevent the white meat from getting dried out while you're waiting for the dark meat to get adequately cooked.

To make a basic brine, combine 2 cups of cool water and 3 tablespoons of coarse kosher salt (use that same proportion to make a larger quantity of brine), stirring to dissolve the salt. Transfer the mixture to a resealable plastic bag, add your meat, and set it aside in the refrigerator. For 1-inch-thick chops or a pork tenderloin, brine for 4 to 6 hours. For a turkey breast, brine for 8 to 12 hours. And for a whole pork loin or whole turkey, brine for 12 to 24 hours (you might need to use a container larger than a resealable bag, then add a plate with something heavy on top to keep the meat submerged).

Remove the meat from the brine (discard the brine), pat it dry, and proceed with your recipe. It's that easy—and it makes such a difference.

is it dry or is it sweet?

It can be hard to tell from the outside of the bottle what the wine inside is going to taste like. But it's especially confounding with both Riesling and Gewürztraminer, which can come in a range of sweetnesses, from super-dry to super-sweet.

Check the label for hints. It might say "dry" or "trocken," which is *dry* in German. It might say "Kabinett" or "Spätlese," which are German terms for off-dry, or very slightly sweet, wines. Or it might say "Auslese," "Beerenauslese," "Eiswein," or "Trockenbeerenauslese," which are German terms for sweet or dessert wines. But often, it won't say anything.

To help combat the confusion, the International Riesling Foundation has developed a graphic to indicate a wine's sweetness level, like you might see on a jar of salsa indicating how hot it is. A few wineries are reportedly starting to use the graphic—meanwhile, consult your retailer.

gewürz-traminer

L ike Riesling, Gewürztraminer (gah-VERTZ-trah-mee-ner) is fruity, bright, fragrant, often floral, and delicious for both sipping and for food and wine pairing. And like Riesling, Gewürztraminer comes in all styles, from dry to very sweet.

But where Riesling is typically light, Gewürz is typically lush and full-bodied, often with riper fruit flavors. Some Gewürztraminers are like a rich, ripe peach—summertime in a glass.

Perhaps best of all are Gewürztraminer's sometimes-notes of cinnamon, anise, allspice, and nutmeg—*Gewürz* is German for "spice"—which open the door to all kinds of interesting and exotic pairing possibilities.

gewürztraminer by another name

Thankfully, with a name that's already a mouthful, there are no others that this wine variety commonly goes by.

pairing with gewürztraminer

Although there are, of course, nuances to Gewürztraminer, the most important factors in food and wine pairing aren't a wine's nuances, but its broad strokes. If you learn a wine's overall characteristics and combine that information with the General Pairing Tips (page 8), you'll have a near-perfect pairing every time.

Broad characteristics:
- dry to off-dry (very slightly sweet)
- medium in acidity, crispness, or brightness
- no or very low tannins
- medium to heavy weight
- medium to strong intensity

(The wine is available much sweeter, but because we're dealing with savory recipes, we're limiting the discussion to dry and off-dry.)

Pairs well with dishes that are:
- not sweet to very slightly sweet
- medium in acidity, crispness, or brightness
- medium to heavy weight
- medium to strong intensity

(Because the wine has no or very low tannins, they're not a factor.)
For example, blue cheese and walnut bread, turkey with apple stuffing, or butternut squash soup.

fine-tuning

As with Riesling, a touch of sweetness in the wine means you can afford only a touch of sweetness in the foods that you pair with it. So add sugary ingredients like fruits and honey judiciously. If you end up with too much sweetness and the wine is tasting sour, add salt and/or acidic ingredients—but try richer ones like buttermilk, yogurt, or sour cream since the wine itself is rich.

In addition to complementing food that's a little sweet, an off-dry Gewürztraminer can taste great with food that's a little spicy.

other nuances

Once you have a pairing that's working on the basis of sweetness, acidity, weight, and intensity, you can start playing with subtler nuances.

Some of the subtle flavors that you might find in a Gewürztraminer include stone fruits, apple, pear, tropical fruits, honey, floral notes, and baking spices. So it works to add those flavors, or foods that complement them, to your dishes.

other thoughts

Some foods that are considered classic pairings with Gewürztraminer are Asian foods (especially richer and moderately spicy dishes like curries); pungent, strong, and even stinky cheeses; sausages and smoked meats; pork and ham; turkey, duck, goose, and other gamier poultry; and rich egg dishes like quiche.

curried pumpkin and potato stew

The hardest thing about making this creamy, coconut milk–laced stew is tackling the pumpkin. Use a sharp knife to cut it into quarters, a spoon to scrape the seeds out of each piece, and then a vegetable peeler to remove the peel. If the pumpkin is proving difficult to quarter, pierce it a few times, then microwave it for a couple of minutes, which will soften it up. After that, it's all downhill, and well worth the effort.

Pair the stew with naan, an Indian flatbread, or toasted pita—to sop up every last drop. • **Serves 6**

2 tablespoons safflower, sunflower, peanut, or other high-heat cooking oil
2 onions (about 1 pound), cut into ¾-inch dice
4 cloves garlic, pressed through a garlic press or minced
2 cups coconut milk (see below)
1 cup reduced-sodium chicken or vegetable broth
2 tablespoons curry powder
2 teaspoons coarse kosher salt, or more to taste
¼ teaspoon ground cinnamon
⅛ teaspoon cayenne pepper
   One 1½-pound sugarpie pumpkin, other cooking pumpkin, or butternut squash, seeded, peeled, and cut into ¾-inch dice (you should have about 4 cups)
1 pound red potatoes, cut into ¾-inch dice
⅓ cup raisins
1 tablespoon fresh lemon juice, or more to taste
½ cup unsweetened shredded or flaked coconut

▓ In a medium stockpot over medium-high heat, warm the oil. Add the onions and cook, stirring occasionally, for 1 minute. Add the garlic and cook, stirring occasionally, until the onions begin to turn translucent, about 2 minutes. Add the coconut milk, broth, curry powder, salt, cinnamon, and cayenne and bring to a boil. Add the pumpkin, potatoes, and raisins and return to a boil. Reduce to a simmer, cover, and cook until the pumpkin and potatoes are tender, about 10 minutes. Remove from the heat and stir in the lemon juice. Taste, ideally with your wine, and add more salt and/or lemon juice if you like.

▓ Serve hot, sprinkled with the coconut.

NOTE Coconut milk is available in the ethnic or Asian section of most major supermarkets. Besides using it in this recipe, you can use coconut milk in Cashew Chicken Stir-Fry (page 88) and in other curries, sauces, and Asian and Asian-inspired dishes. It's also great in rice pudding.

onion and apple tart

This tart is a stunner, with sweetness from caramelized onions and apple, warm spice from nutmeg, and a creamy custard filling holding it all together. • **Serves 6 to 8**

4 tablespoons (½ stick) unsalted butter
2 onions (about 1 pound), halved lengthwise and thinly sliced
2 teaspoons coarse kosher salt
½ teaspoon freshly ground black pepper
 Pastry dough for one 11-inch tart or 9-inch deep-dish pie, homemade or store-bought
3 large eggs
1 cup heavy whipping cream
1½ teaspoons ground nutmeg, preferably freshly grated
1 sweet-tart baking apple, such as McIntosh or Jonathan
 Special equipment: 11-inch fluted tart pan (1⅛ inches deep) with a removable bottom

▥ In a large skillet over medium heat, melt the butter. Add the onions, salt, and pepper and cook, stirring occasionally, until soft, about 5 minutes. Reduce the heat to very low and cook, stirring occasionally, until the onions are pale gold, about 20 minutes. Set aside to cool. (You can prepare the onions in advance, storing them covered in the refrigerator for up to 3 days or in the freezer for several months. Return them to room temperature before proceeding.)

▥ On a lightly floured surface, roll out the dough to a 14-inch circle. Fit the dough into an 11-inch fluted tart pan (1⅛ inches deep) with a removable bottom. Trim the excess to a ½-inch overhang, then fold the overhang back into the pan to reinforce the fluted edge. Using a fork, pierce the bottom of the pastry all over. Refrigerate for 30 minutes. (You can refrigerate the pastry, covered, for up to a day.)

▥ Preheat the oven to 400°F.

▥ Place the chilled tart shell on a rimmed baking sheet and line the shell with foil and pie weights. Bake until the pastry is set and pale gold along the rim, 15 to 20 minutes. Carefully remove the foil and weights and continue baking until the shell is golden all over, 10 to 15 minutes.

▥ Meanwhile, in a medium bowl, whisk together the eggs, cream, and nutmeg. Stir in the onions. Peel, core, and thinly slice the apple.

▥ Remove the shell from the oven (leave the oven on). Pour the egg mixture into the shell and arrange the apple slices decoratively on top. Press on the apples to slightly submerge them. Bake until the top is lightly browned, the apples are tender, and the center is set, 25 to 35 minutes. Let the tart stand for 10 minutes before slicing and serving.

cashew chicken stir-fry

Stir-fry is one of my favorite weeknight dishes because, after a little prep, dinner is on the table in a jiffy. This particular version is especially indulgent, with both cashews and coconut milk giving it a soft, silky quality that's a natural for Gewürztraminer. ▪ **Serves 4**

 1 cup basmati rice
 ¾ cup coconut milk (see note on page 85)
 ½ cup reduced-sodium chicken broth
 ¼ cup aji-mirin sweet cooking rice seasoning (Japanese cooking wine) (see note on page 70)
 3 tablespoons soy sauce
 ½ teaspoon dried crushed red pepper flakes
 12 ounces boneless, skinless chicken thighs, cut into 1-inch pieces
 2 teaspoons cornstarch dissolved in 1 tablespoon cold water
 2 tablespoons safflower, sunflower, peanut, or other high-heat cooking oil
 2 carrots, cut diagonally into ⅛-inch slices
 4 cloves garlic, pressed through a garlic press or minced
   One ½-inch piece fresh ginger, peeled and finely chopped
   One 8-ounce can sliced water chestnuts, drained
 8 scallions, white and light green parts only, halved lengthwise and cut into 1-inch pieces
 ¾ cup roasted, salted cashews

▦ Cook the rice according to package directions. Remove from the heat and let it stand, covered, until ready to serve.

▦ In a medium bowl, combine the coconut milk, broth, aji-mirin, soy sauce, and red pepper flakes. Add the chicken, tossing to coat, and set aside for 15 minutes. Drain the chicken, saving the marinade. Stir the cornstarch mixture into the marinade and set aside.

▦ In a large wok or skillet over high heat, warm the oil. Add the chicken and cook, stirring, until cooked through, 3 to 4 minutes. Use a slotted spoon to transfer the chicken to a plate. Set aside.

▦ Add the carrots to the wok and cook, stirring, until crisp-tender, 2 to 3 minutes. Add the garlic and ginger and cook, stirring, until fragrant, about 30 seconds. Add the chicken, water chestnuts, scallions, cashews, and marinade mixture and cook, stirring occasionally, until the sauce comes to a boil and thickens, about 1 minute.

▦ Arrange the rice on a platter or plates and top with the stir-fry mixture, dividing it evenly. Serve hot.

FOOD + WINE TIP Gewürztraminer is a natural for a rich stir-fry like this one. For lighter Asian foods, like Thai or Vietnamese dishes, or sushi, go with Riesling.

yogurt chicken with chutney yogurt sauce

Don't let the simplicity of this recipe fool you—it has layers of warm, complex flavor. Get it started in advance of serving, though, so the chicken has ample time to marinate. ▪ **Serves 6**

- 2 cups plain yogurt (low-fat is okay)
- 4 cloves garlic, pressed through a garlic press or minced
- ½ teaspoon coarse kosher salt
- ¼ teaspoon freshly ground black pepper
- ¼ teaspoon ground cinnamon
- ¼ teaspoon ground cloves
- ¼ teaspoon ground cumin
- ⅛ teaspoon ground allspice
- ⅛ teaspoon ground cardamom
- ⅛ teaspoon ground coriander
- 6 chicken leg quarters or 6 legs and 6 thighs
- ⅓ cup mango chutney

░ In a medium bowl, combine the yogurt, garlic, salt, pepper, cinnamon, cloves, cumin, allspice, cardamom, and coriander. (You can prepare the yogurt mixture up to 3 days in advance, storing it covered in the refrigerator.)

░ Divide the chicken between two large resealable bags. Add ½ cup of the yogurt mixture to each bag and seal, squeezing out as much air as possible. Set the chicken aside in the refrigerator for 6 to 12 hours, turning occasionally. Refrigerate the remaining yogurt mixture.

░ Preheat the oven to 400°F.

░ Arrange the chicken on a rimmed baking sheet, squeezing the yogurt mixture out of the bag and over the chicken. Bake for 45 minutes, until cooked through.

░ Meanwhile, in the bowl of a food processor, combine the remaining yogurt mixture and the chutney and pulse to chop the chutney.

░ Serve the chicken hot, with the chutney yogurt mixture spooned on top.

FOOD + WINE TIP If you like things with a little kick, use hot mango chutney in this recipe—the warmth nicely complements the spicy notes in the wine.

monster hot turkey sandwiches with muenster horseradish "gravy"

Here's a riff on the classic diner hot turkey sandwich, only better, thanks to a thick slice of flavorful sourdough bread, a hint of tart-sweet cranberries, and a molten, cheesy sauce with a fabulous horseradish kick. The recipe would be a great way to use up leftover Thanksgiving turkey—but don't wait until then to enjoy it. ▪ **Serves 4**

2	tablespoons (¼ stick) unsalted butter
¼	onion, cut into ¼-inch dice
2	tablespoons all-purpose flour
1½	cups milk (low-fat is okay)
2	ounces Muenster cheese, shredded (you should have about ⅔ cup)
1	tablespoon prepared horseradish, or more to taste
1½	teaspoons coarse kosher salt
½	cup cranberry sauce
	Four ¾-inch-thick slices crusty artisan sourdough bread, cut on a diagonal, if necessary, to make sandwich-sized slices
1	pound sliced roast turkey, room temperature

▓ In a medium saucepan over medium heat, melt the butter. Add the onion and cook, stirring occasionally, until tender, 2 to 3 minutes. Sprinkle in the flour and cook, whisking constantly, for 1 minute. Slowly add the milk, whisking out any lumps of flour, and cook, stirring occasionally, until the sauce thickens and comes to a simmer, 1 to 2 minutes. Remove from the heat and stir in the cheese, horseradish, and salt, gently stirring until the cheese is melted. Taste, ideally with your wine, and add more horseradish if you like. Cover to keep warm and set aside.

▓ Spread the cranberry sauce on one side of the bread. Top with the turkey and arrange on plates. Spoon the sauce over the sandwiches, dividing it evenly, and serve.

roast turkey with pan gravy and spiced sausage dressing

It can be a challenge choosing a wine to serve with Thanksgiving dinner. The turkey and gravy are savory, but the yams and cranberry sauce are sweet. Gewürztraminer covers the gamut terrifically, and even goes the meal one better, with the baking spice flavors in the wine complementing similar flavors often in the meal.

Note that in this recipe, brining the turkey is absolutely optional, but it's highly recommended to help produce a flavorful, juicy bird. The process described below is basically the same as the one described on page 81, but it adds some sugar, along with a few details that are useful when brining something as large as a turkey. If you do choose to brine, it's especially important to use reduced-sodium broth for your gravy. • **Serves 8 to 10, with leftovers**

FOR THE DRESSING

 1 pound sweet Italian sausage, casings removed
 4 tablespoons (½ stick) unsalted butter, divided
 1 large red bell pepper, cored, seeded, and cut into ½-inch dice
 1 large red onion, cut into ½-inch dice
 1 pound crusty artisan French or Italian bread, with crusts,
   cut or torn into ¾-inch pieces (you should have about 16 cups)
 12 scallions, white and light green parts only, cut into ¼-inch pieces
 1½ teaspoons coarse kosher salt
 1½ teaspoons ground ginger
 ¾ teaspoon freshly ground black pepper
 ½ teaspoon ground allspice
 ½ teaspoon ground cinnamon
 ½ teaspoon ground nutmeg, preferably freshly grated
 ¼ teaspoon ground cloves
 2 cups reduced-sodium chicken broth

FOR THE TURKEY

 3 cups coarse kosher salt (optional, for brining)
 1 cup sugar (optional, for brining)
   One 12- to 14-pound turkey, thawed, neck and giblets removed
 3 to 4 tablespoons extra virgin olive oil
 2 cups coarse kosher salt (if you don't brine)
 1 tablespoon freshly ground black pepper
   About 2 cups reduced-sodium chicken broth

FOR THE GRAVY

   Pan drippings from roast turkey
   About ¼ cup all-purpose flour
 1 cup Gewürztraminer, or other dry or off-dry white wine (optional)
 1 to 2 cups reduced-sodium chicken broth
 1 teaspoon coarse kosher salt, or more to taste
 ½ teaspoon freshly ground black pepper, or more to taste

(continued on following page)

To make the dressing: In a large skillet over medium heat, cook the sausage, stirring occasionally and breaking up the pieces, until browned and cooked through, 8 to 10 minutes. Use a slotted spoon to transfer the sausage to a large bowl.

Add 2 tablespoons of the butter to the skillet and melt over medium heat. Add the bell pepper and onion and cook, stirring occasionally, until very tender, 8 to 10 minutes. Transfer the mixture to the bowl with the sausage. Add the bread, scallions, salt, ginger, black pepper, allspice, cinnamon, nutmeg, and cloves to the bowl. Add the broth, gently stirring to evenly moisten.

Spoon the dressing into a 9 x 13-inch baking pan. Cut the remaining 2 tablespoons of butter into pea-sized pieces and dot them over the top. (You can prepare the dressing up to 2 days in advance. Cool it thoroughly, then store it covered in the refrigerator. Return it to room temperature before proceeding.)

To make the turkey: If you want to brine the turkey, in a container large enough to hold the turkey, combine the salt, sugar, and 2 gallons of cold water, whisking to dissolve the salt and sugar. Add the turkey and, if necessary, a plate with something heavy on top to keep the turkey submerged. After 12 to 24 hours, remove the turkey from the brine, rinse it inside and out with cold water, and pat it dry.

(If you don't have a container large enough to hold the turkey, or if a turkey in a container won't fit in your refrigerator, place the turkey in a double layer of heavy-duty, unscented, nonrecycled plastic bags. Pour in the brine solution and seal the bag, squeezing out as much air as possible. Place the bag in an ice chest and add frozen ice packs. Change or add the ice packs as necessary to maintain a temperature of 38° to 40°F in the ice chest.)

Preheat the oven to 400°F.

Rub the turkey all over with the olive oil. Sprinkle inside and out with the 2 tablespoons of salt (if you didn't brine) and the black pepper. Tie the legs together (if they aren't already) and tuck in the wings. Arrange the turkey, breast side up, on a roasting rack set in a roasting pan. Add about ¼ inch of broth to the bottom of the pan. Loosely cover the turkey with foil and roast for 1 hour.

░░ Remove the foil and baste the turkey with the pan juices. Continue roasting, uncovered, basting every 20 or 30 minutes, until an internal thermometer inserted into the thickest part of the thigh without touching the bone reads 165°F, 2 to 2¾ hours total cooking time. (If the pan gets dry, pour in more broth or water to maintain about ¼ inch of liquid. If any part of the turkey gets too brown, cover it loosely with foil.) Transfer the turkey to a cutting board and let it rest, loosely covered with foil, for 20 to 30 minutes. (It will continue to cook, reaching an internal temperature of about 180°F.)

░░ About 15 minutes before the turkey is done, cover the dressing with foil, add it to the oven, and bake until heated through, about 30 minutes. (If there isn't room in the oven, either use a second 400°F oven or wait until the turkey is done to bake the dressing.) Uncover and bake until the top is crisp and golden, about 20 minutes.

░░ While the turkey is resting and the dressing is still baking, make the gravy: Pour the pan drippings into a large measuring cup or other container. Set the mixture aside for a few minutes to let the fat rise to the top. Skim the fat into a separate container (don't discard the fat).

░░ Place the roasting pan over low heat, straddled over two burners if necessary, and add ¼ cup of the skimmed fat. Once the fat is hot, sprinkle in the flour and cook, whisking constantly, until the flour is lightly toasted and the mixture is smooth, about 5 minutes. Stir in the wine or 1 cup of the broth, scraping up the browned bits on the bottom of the pan. Add the pan drippings, stirring in a little at a time, and then the broth as necessary, until the gravy reaches the desired texture.

░░ Remove the gravy from the heat and stir in the salt and black pepper. Taste, ideally with your wine, and add more salt and/or black pepper if you like.

░░ Carve the turkey and serve it hot, with the gravy and dressing on the side.

FOOD + WINE TIP Another good choice to pair with turkey and all the trimmings is Pinot Noir—but only if your side dishes aren't too sweet.

duck à l'abricot

This tasty twist on duck à l'orange is inspired by the stone fruit flavors often found in Gewürztraminer. If you've never roasted a whole duck, give it a try. It's just as simple as roasting a chicken, but because duck is less expected, the ultimate dish is more exciting, dramatic, and impressive.

On the side, try wild rice, roasted yams, or pureed winter squash.

Serves 4

- 1 teaspoon ground cardamom
- 1 teaspoon ground cumin
- ½ teaspoon ground ginger
- 2 teaspoons coarse kosher salt, divided, or more to taste
- ¾ teaspoon freshly ground black pepper, divided, or more to taste
  One 5- to 6-pound whole duck
  One 1-inch piece fresh ginger, cut into 4 pieces, plus ½ teaspoon freshly grated ginger
- ½ cup apricot nectar
- ¼ cup all-fruit apricot preserves
- 3 tablespoons Gewürztraminer, or other dry or off-dry white wine
- 4 teaspoons rice vinegar
- 8 shallots, halved lengthwise
- 16 dried apricot halves, halved

▓ Preheat the oven to 475°F.

▓ In a small bowl, combine the cardamom, cumin, ground ginger, 1½ teaspoons of the salt, and ½ teaspoon of the pepper. Use the tip of a sharp paring knife to prick the duck all over, cutting into the skin on a diagonal to avoid cutting into the meat. Sprinkle the duck inside and out with the spice mixture. Place the pieces of fresh ginger inside the duck. Tie the legs together and tuck in the wings. Arrange the duck, breast side up, on a rack in a 9 x 13-inch baking pan. Add about ¼ inch of water to the bottom of the pan and roast for 30 minutes.

▓ Meanwhile, in a small saucepan over high heat, combine the apricot nectar, apricot preserves, wine, vinegar, grated ginger, remaining ½ teaspoon of salt, and remaining ¼ teaspoon of pepper and bring to a boil. Cook, stirring occasionally, until the mixture is slightly thickened, about 3 minutes (adjust the heat, if necessary, to avoid boiling over). Divide the mixture in half and set both halves aside.

▓ After the duck has cooked for 30 minutes, reduce the oven to 350°F and brush the duck all over with some of one half of the apricot nectar mixture. Scatter the shallots around the duck and continue roasting for 15 minutes.

⫶ Scatter the apricots around the duck and brush with the same half of the apricot mixture. Continue roasting, brushing every 15 or 20 minutes, until an internal thermometer inserted into the thickest part of the thigh without touching the bone reads 165°F for medium, 1½ to 1¾ hours total cooking time. (If the pan gets dry, pour in more water to maintain about ¼ inch of liquid. If any part of the duck gets too brown, cover it loosely with foil.) Transfer the duck to a cutting board and let it rest, loosely covered with foil, for 15 minutes. (It will continue to cook, reaching an internal temperature of about 175°F.)

⫶ Meanwhile, drain the shallot and apricot mixture in the roasting pan, straining the liquid. Stir the mixture (discard the liquid) into the other half of the apricot nectar mixture. Taste, ideally with your wine, and add more salt and/or pepper if you like. Set aside.

⫶ Carve the duck and serve it hot, with the shallots, apricots, and their juices on the side.

sticky asian barbecued baby back ribs

Have plenty of napkins on hand—although you might prefer not to use them. These ribs are truly finger-lickin' good.

Note that the ribs need to be started about a day in advance of serving. • **Serves 4**

　2 racks pork baby back ribs (3 to 4 pounds)
　1 cup aji-mirin sweet cooking rice seasoning (Japanese cooking wine) (see note on page 70)
　1 cup soy sauce
　½ cup rice vinegar
　¼ cup sesame oil
　4 teaspoons Chinese five-spice powder (see note on page 98)
　6 cloves garlic, smashed
　6 tablespoons packed light brown sugar
　2 tablespoons cornstarch dissolved in 3 tablespoons cold water
　3 scallions, white and light green parts only, thinly sliced
1½ teaspoons sesame seeds, toasted (see note on page 49)

▓ Preheat the oven to 250°F.

▓ Meanwhile, from the back, boney side of the ribs, slide a thin, blunt tool, such as a flathead screwdriver, over the bone but under the thin membrane that covers the entire back of the rack. Work the tool down the bone, swaying from side to side, until there's a gap large enough for you to grab the membrane and peel it off. Place the ribs in a large roasting pan (you can cut the racks into pieces if need be). Set aside.

▓ In a medium saucepan over medium-high heat, combine the aji-mirin, soy sauce, vinegar, sesame oil, Chinese five-spice powder, and garlic and bring to a boil. Pour the mixture over the ribs, cover (tight-fitting foil is fine if you don't have a lid), and bake until the meat is tender and almost falling off the bones, about 2 hours. Remove from the oven and let the ribs cool in the sauce. Refrigerate for 12 to 24 hours.

▓ Remove the ribs from the baking liquid (save the liquid), scraping the fat off the ribs. Cut each rack into 3- or 4-rib pieces and set aside. Skim the fat off the liquid. Strain 1½ cups of the liquid and set aside (discard the remaining liquid).

▓ In a medium saucepan over medium heat, combine the strained baking liquid with the brown sugar and the cornstarch mixture, whisking to dissolve the sugar. Bring to a boil, stirring, until thickened, 1 to 2 minutes. Remove from the heat and set aside.

(continued on following page)

▥ Prepare the grill to medium heat and lightly oil the grate. Grill the ribs until heated through, 2 to 3 minutes per side. Brush both sides with some of the brown sugar sauce and cook until the sauce is browned in spots, 1 to 2 minutes per side.

▥ Transfer the ribs to a platter or plates and sprinkle with the scallions and sesame seeds. Serve hot, with the remaining brown sugar sauce on the side.

NOTE **Chinese five-spice powder** is available in either the spice section or in the ethnic or Asian section of most major supermarkets. Besides using it in this recipe, you can use it in Hoisin Pork Tenderloin with Asian Salad (page 78), sprinkle it onto roasted meats and vegetables, and stir it into rice.

an argument for off-dry

I said it in the first *100 Perfect Pairings* cookbook and I'll say it again: I don't know how or why off-dry wines became so unhip, but they absolutely shouldn't be. Because not only can an off-dry wine be more pleasant to drink, but it often goes better with food.

Why? Because many savory dishes, like barbecued chicken and sweet-and-sour stir-fry, have a touch of sweetness. And, per General Pairing Tip 1 (page 8), a similar sweetness in the wine will help prevent the food from making the wine taste sour.

In fact, many of today's hippest cuisines—Thai, Latin, Indian, Moroccan—have elements of sweetness or spiciness that make them ideal for off-dry wines.

honey-orange lamb chops

The same sauce would be good on chicken or pork, but it's most interesting with lamb, the fruity flavors of the orange playing off the stronger flavors of the meat. • **Serves 2**

- ½ small orange, cut into 6 chunks
- ¼ cup white or golden balsamic vinegar (see note on page 23)
- 2 tablespoons honey
- ¼ teaspoon ground allspice
- 1 teaspoon coarse kosher salt, divided
- 8 lamb rib chops, about ¾ inch thick, or 1 rack of lamb cut into 8 chops, about ¾ inch thick
- ½ teaspoon freshly ground black pepper, divided

▒ In the bowl of a food processor, combine the orange (peel and all), vinegar, honey, allspice, and ½ teaspoon of the salt and pulse to make a coarse puree, scraping down the bowl as necessary. Divide the mixture in half and set both halves aside. (You can prepare the orange mixture up to a day in advance, storing it covered in the refrigerator.)

▒ Preheat the broiler. Arrange a rack 6 inches from the heat. Oil a rimmed baking sheet with safflower, sunflower, peanut, or other high-heat cooking oil.

▒ Place the lamb on the baking sheet and brush with some of one half of the orange mixture. Sprinkle with ¼ teaspoon of the remaining salt and ¼ teaspoon of the pepper. Broil for 4 minutes. Turn and brush again with the orange mixture. Sprinkle with the remaining ¼ teaspoon of salt and remaining ¼ teaspoon of pepper. Broil for 4 minutes for medium rare or 5 minutes for medium.

▒ Let the chops rest, loosely covered with foil, for 5 minutes. Serve hot, with the other half of the orange mixture on the side.

FOOD + WINE TIP It's a little edgy to pair lamb with white wine. But there are two reasons it works here. One, because lamb is much milder than it used to be, so it doesn't require a red to balance a strong flavor. And two, because when it comes to food and wine pairing, what dresses up the dish is almost always more important than the main ingredient. And here, the sauce leans toward a white.

rosé

Perhaps you think Rosé passé—too faddy, too soda pop-y, too sweet, too yesterday.

But Rosé is in fact quite de rigueur. These days, it's showing up everywhere, from the wine lists of trendy restaurants to the picnic tables of master sommeliers. These new Rosés are more in the European style and generally drier than those popular in the U.S. a few years ago—all in all, they're beautifully crafted wines that deliciously combine mild red wine flavors with a refreshing, best-served-cold lightness.

For food and wine pairing, this is great news, because Rosé is ideal for the simply prepared, Mediterranean-inspired foods that have increasingly become American cuisine. It also works with barbecue and grilled dishes, mildly spicy or smoky foods, and many ethnic cuisines.

So I say, vive la Rosé!

rosé by another name
• **Rosato, Rosado.** These are the Italian and Spanish names, respectively, for Rosé. • **Vin Gris.** Literally "gray wine," a French name for very pale Rosés. Vin Gris is often made from Pinot Noir grapes. • **Blush.** Originally, this was a name for very pale Rosés, à la Vin Gris, but it's come to simply be another generic term for Rosé. • **White Zinfandel, White Grenache, White Merlot, etc.** These are U.S. names for Rosés made from specific grapes—Zinfandel, Grenache, Merlot, etc.

pairing with rosé
Although there are, of course, nuances to Rosé, the most important factors in food and wine pairing aren't a wine's nuances, but its broad strokes. If you learn a wine's overall characteristics and combine that information with the General Pairing Tips (page 8), you'll have a near-perfect pairing every time.

Broad characteristics:
• dry to off-dry (very slightly sweet)
• medium in acidity, crispness, or brightness
• no or very low tannins
• light to medium weight
• light to medium intensity

Pairs well with dishes that are:
- not sweet to very slightly sweet
- medium in acidity, crispness, or brightness
- light to medium weight
- light to medium intensity

(Because the wine has no or very low tannins, they're not a factor.)
For example, shrimp salad, a turkey sandwich with cranberry sauce, or barbecued chicken.

fine-tuning

As with Riesling and Gewürztraminer, a touch of sweetness in the wine means you can afford a touch of sweetness in the food. If, however, you end up with too much sweetness and it's making the wine taste sour, try adding acidic ingredients, but use ones that are light, bright, and fruity like the wine—for example, lemon and lime juice, apple cider vinegar, and red wine vinegar.

In addition to complementing food that's a little sweet, an off-dry Rosé can taste great with food that's a little spicy.

And remember that you can complement the fruitiness of Rosé not only by judiciously adding fruit to your dishes, but also by adding fruity elements, like citrus zest, fruit-infused vinegars and oils, and even dried fruits, which tend to be less sweet than their fresh counterparts.

other nuances

Once you have a pairing that's working on the basis of sweetness, acidity, weight, and intensity, you can start playing with subtler nuances.

Some of the subtle flavors that you might find in a Rosé include red berries (especially raspberries, strawberries, and cranberries), cherries, pomegranate, grapefruit, and floral notes. So it works to add those flavors, or foods that complement them, to your dishes.

other thoughts

Some foods that are considered classic pairings with Rosé are deli meats, picnic foods, poultry, pork, fish and shellfish (especially grilled), barbecue and barbecue sauce, salads, and Mediterranean food.

my big fat greek salad

This recipe goes the classic Greek salad one better, adding extras like garbanzos and marinated artichoke hearts, plus crispy pita chips to enjoy alongside. • **Serves 4**

    3 tablespoons red wine vinegar
    1 tablespoon Dijon mustard
    3 cloves garlic, pressed through a garlic press or minced
    1 teaspoon coarse kosher salt
    ½ teaspoon freshly ground black pepper
    6 tablespoons extra virgin olive oil, divided
    1 round pita bread, white, wheat, or ½ of each for variety
    1 head iceberg lettuce, cut or torn into bite-sized pieces (you should have
      about 12 cups)
      One 14.75-ounce jar marinated artichoke hearts, drained and halved lengthwise
   12 ounces feta cheese, cut into ¾-inch cubes (you should have 2½ to 3 cups)
      One 8.75-ounce can garbanzo beans, drained and rinsed
    2 tomatoes, cut into ¾-inch dice
    1 small cucumber, peeled and cut into ¾-inch dice
    ¾ cup pitted kalamata olives
    ¼ red onion, thinly sliced
   12 pepperoncini peppers
    1 tablespoon chopped fresh flat-leaf parsley
    1 tablespoon chopped fresh oregano

▨ In a small bowl, combine the vinegar, mustard, garlic, salt, and black pepper, whisking to dissolve the salt. Whisk in 5 tablespoons of the olive oil. Set aside. (You can prepare the dressing up to 3 days in advance, storing it covered in the refrigerator.)

▨ Preheat the oven to 375°F.

▨ Cut the pita in half. Split each half into 2 semicircles. Cut each semicircle into 3 wedges. Arrange the wedges on a baking sheet, smooth side down, and brush with the remaining 1 tablespoon of olive oil. Bake until lightly toasted, 6 to 8 minutes. Set aside to cool slightly.

▨ While the pitas are baking, in a large bowl, combine the lettuce with about half of the dressing. Transfer the mixture to a platter or plates. Arrange the artichoke hearts, cheese, garbanzo beans, tomatoes, cucumber, olives, and onion on the lettuce, dividing them evenly. Arrange the pepperoncini peppers around the salad. Sprinkle with the parsley and oregano, drizzle with the remaining dressing, and serve, with the toasted pitas on the side.

FOOD + WINE TIP Because of the vinaigrette dressing, this salad would also pair well with Sauvignon Blanc or Pinot Grigio.

chile and cheese pie

Sort of a southwestern quiche, this cheesy pie would be great for lunch, brunch, or dinner. Serve it with a tomato and cilantro salad or a cup of gazpacho. • **Serves 6**

  2 tablespoons extra virgin olive oil
  ½ red bell pepper, cored, seeded, and cut into ¼-inch slices
  ½ yellow bell pepper, cored, seeded, and cut into ¼-inch slices
  1 small red onion, halved and cut into ¼-inch slices
    Pastry dough for one 11-inch tart or 9-inch deep-dish pie, homemade or store-bought
  3 large eggs
  1 cup crème fraîche
  ½ cup heavy whipping cream
    One 8-ounce package shredded Cheddar and Monterey Jack cheese blend
    One 7-ounce can whole green chiles, drained and cut into ¼-inch slices
  2 teaspoons coarse kosher salt
    Special equipment: 9-inch deep-dish pie pan (1½ inches deep)

▥ In a large skillet over medium-high heat, warm the olive oil. Add the bell peppers and cook, stirring occasionally, for 2 minutes. Add the onion and cook, stirring occasionally, until the vegetables are tender, 4 to 5 minutes. Set aside to cool. (You can prepare the bell peppers and onions in advance, storing them covered in the refrigerator for up to 3 days or in the freezer for several months. Return them to room temperature before proceeding.)

▥ On a lightly floured surface, roll out the dough to a 13-inch circle. Fit the dough into a 9-inch deep-dish pie pan (1½ inches deep). Trim the excess to a 1-inch overhang, then fold the overhang under and shape a decorative rim. Using a fork, pierce the bottom of the pastry all over. Refrigerate for 30 minutes. (You can refrigerate the pastry, covered, for up to a day.)

▥ Preheat the oven to 375°F.

▥ Place the chilled pie shell on a baking sheet and line the shell with foil and pie weights. Bake until the pastry is set and pale gold along the rim, 20 to 25 minutes.

▥ Meanwhile, in a large bowl, whisk together the eggs, crème fraîche, and cream. Stir in the cheese, chiles, and salt. Stir in the bell peppers and onions.

▥ Carefully remove the foil and weights from the shell (leave the oven on). Pour in the egg mixture and bake until the top is golden and the center is set, 40 to 45 minutes. Let the pie stand for 10 minutes before slicing and serving.

tex-mex turkey meatloaf with corn salsa

A happy twist on the usual, this meatloaf is especially good in the summertime, when peak-of-season corn and tomatoes are at their flavorful best. • **Serves 6**

  1 ear fresh corn, husked
½ red bell pepper, cored, seeded, and cut into ¼-inch dice
  3 tablespoons chopped fresh cilantro, plus sprigs for garnish
  2 tablespoons fresh lime juice (1 or 2 limes)
  4 tomatoes, cored, seeded, and cut into ¼-inch dice, divided
  1 red onion, cut into ¼-inch dice, divided
  4 cloves garlic, pressed through a garlic press or minced, divided
5½ teaspoons coarse kosher salt, divided
  2 pounds ground turkey
  1 cup crushed corn tortilla chips (about 3 ounces), plus whole chips for serving
  3 large eggs, lightly beaten
  1 tablespoon ground coriander
  1 tablespoon ground cumin
  1 teaspoon freshly ground black pepper

▧ Use a small, sharp knife to remove the kernels from the corn. In a medium bowl, combine the corn, bell pepper, chopped cilantro, lime juice, one-half of the tomatoes, one-quarter of the onion, one-quarter of the garlic, and 1½ teaspoons of the salt. (You can prepare the salsa up to 4 hours in advance, storing it covered in the refrigerator.)

▧ Preheat the oven to 375°F.

▧ In a large bowl, combine the turkey, crushed tortilla chips, eggs, coriander, cumin, black pepper, remaining tomatoes, remaining onion, remaining garlic, and remaining 4 teaspoons of salt, mixing gently until just combined.

▧ Gently pack the mixture into a 9 x 5 x 3-inch loaf pan. Place the pan on a rimmed baking sheet and bake until an internal thermometer inserted into the center reads 165°F, about 1 hour.

▧ Turn on the broiler and arrange a rack so that the top of the meat-loaf is about 6 inches from the heat. Broil until the top of the meatloaf is browned, 3 to 5 minutes. Let it rest for 10 minutes. (It will continue to cook, reaching an internal temperature of about 175°F.)

▧ Slice the meatloaf and serve hot, with the salsa and cilantro sprigs on top and whole tortilla chips on the side.

FOOD + WINE TIP Because tortilla chips can vary in saltiness, so can the dish. If your wine is tasting sour—which might especially be the case with a dry Rosé—add a little salt to the meatloaf at the table.

roasted vegetable and goat cheese sandwiches

This sandwich would be great for a picnic because you can prepare it in advance without worrying about the fillings making the bread soggy. Plus, the summery flavors are perfect for a warm afternoon, accompanied, of course, by ideal-for-warm-weather Rosé.

In the unlikely event that you have leftovers, enjoy the sandwiches reheated in the oven. The bread will get crispy, the cheese will get warm, and you'll get to savor the delicious flavors all over again.

• Serves 6

2 pounds eggplant, cut into ½-inch dice (you should have about 9 cups)
2 red bell peppers, cored, seeded, and cut into ½-inch dice
¼ cup extra virgin olive oil
2 teaspoons coarse kosher salt
½ teaspoon freshly ground black pepper
1½ cups chèvre (spreadable goat cheese) (about 12 ounces)
2 tablespoons fresh lemon juice
1 tablespoon chopped fresh marjoram (see below)
¼ teaspoon dried crushed red pepper flakes
6 crusty seeded sandwich rolls, split horizontally

■ Preheat the oven to 375°F.

■ In a large bowl, combine the eggplant, bell peppers, olive oil, salt, and black pepper, tossing to coat. Arrange the mixture in a single layer on 2 rimmed baking sheets and roast until the vegetables are tender, about 30 minutes.

■ Meanwhile, in a medium bowl, combine the cheese, lemon juice, marjoram, and red pepper flakes. (You can prepare the eggplant and cheese mixtures up to 2 days in advance, storing them covered in the refrigerator. Return them to room temperature before proceeding.)

■ Remove the soft bread from the bottom halves of the rolls, making a cavity in each half for the eggplant mixture. Fill the cavities with the eggplant mixture, dividing it evenly, pressing it in and mounding it over the cavities. Spread the cheese mixture on the bready side of the top halves of the rolls, dividing it evenly. Place the top halves of the rolls on the bottom halves. Serve warm or room temperature.

NOTE **Fresh marjoram** is available in the produce section of many supermarkets. Besides using it in this recipe, you can use it in Smoky Lentil and Vegetable Stew (page 160), and in soups, stews, salad dressings, and almost any place that you'd use fresh oregano. If you can't find fresh marjoram, substitute equal parts fresh oregano and fresh sage.

roast salmon and potatoes with romesco sauce

A version of this dish is part of my regular repertoire. Sometimes I grill the salmon and potatoes instead of roasting them, and sometimes I swap the salmon for chicken, but I always use a forkful of potato to wipe up every last bit of the seductive Spanish red pepper sauce.

• **Serves 4**

16 small red potatoes (about 1½ pounds), halved
 3 tablespoons extra virgin olive oil, divided
2½ teaspoons coarse kosher salt, divided
 1 teaspoon freshly ground black pepper, divided
   Four 6-ounce salmon fillets, about ¾ inch thick, skin removed if you like
   About 1 cup Romesco Sauce (recipe follows)

▨ Preheat the oven to 450°F. Arrange one rack in the bottom third of the oven and another in the top third.

▨ In a large bowl, combine the potatoes, 2 tablespoons of the olive oil, 1½ teaspoons of the salt, and ½ teaspoon of the pepper, tossing to thoroughly and evenly coat. Arrange the potatoes on a rimmed baking sheet and roast on the top rack until tender, about 15 minutes.

▨ Meanwhile, brush the salmon with the remaining 1 tablespoon of olive oil and sprinkle with the remaining 1 teaspoon of salt and remaining ½ teaspoon of pepper. Arrange the salmon on a rimmed baking sheet.

▨ Toss the potatoes and return them to the top rack. Place the salmon on the bottom rack and roast until the salmon is cooked through and the potatoes are browned, about 8 minutes.

▨ Arrange the salmon on a platter or plates with the potatoes on the side. Drape the romesco sauce on top and serve hot.

romesco sauce · **Makes about 3 cups**

This recipe makes more romesco than you'll need for the salmon and potatoes recipe on the previous page, but leftover romesco is a very, very good thing. I like to freeze it in an ice cube tray, pop the frozen cubes into a resealable bag, and stash it back in the freezer. Then it's readily available to use as a pizza sauce, as sandwich spread, or simply to dress up an otherwise ordinary grilled chicken beast.

¾ cup drained jarred roasted red peppers or piquillo peppers
4 ounces slivered almonds (about ⅞ cup), toasted (see note on page 18)
3 ounces French or Italian bread, with crusts, cut or torn into 1-inch pieces (you should have about 2 cups)
3 cloves garlic
5 tablespoons sherry vinegar or red wine vinegar, or more to taste
2 tablespoons brandy
2 tablespoons smoked paprika (see note on page 73)
1 tablespoon tomato paste
1½ teaspoons coarse kosher salt, or more to taste
¼ teaspoon cayenne pepper
1 cup extra virgin olive oil

In the bowl of a food processor, combine the red peppers, almonds, bread, and garlic and pulse to coarsely chop, scraping down the bowl as necessary. Add the vinegar, brandy, paprika, tomato paste, salt, and cayenne and process to a coarse paste, scraping down the bowl as necessary. With the motor running, slowly add the olive oil and process until smooth, scraping down the bowl as necessary. Taste, ideally with your wine, and add more vinegar and/or salt if you like. (You can prepare the romesco sauce in advance, storing it in the refrigerator for up to a week or in the freezer for several months.)

two tips for wine tasting

1 Whether you're trying wines in a winery tasting room, a retail shop, or even at your own dinner table, the temptation is to take a sip and ask yourself, "Do I like this?" But the answer could be "no" simply because many wines don't taste good on their own—they need food to help them really sing. Instead, ask yourself, "What food would this be good with?" You'll find that there's something to appreciate about almost every wine and, in the process, you'll hone your food and wine pairing skills.

2 Another wine-tasting temptation is to compare wines, to notice how they're different. Instead, use the opportunity to notice what they have in common—what this Rosé, for example, has in common with others at the table, and with what you know about Rosé as a whole. You'll end up adding to your knowledge of all Rosés, which will be useful when considering buying one, any one.

tilapia with gazpacho salsa

Here's everything you love about the cold Spanish soup in a chunky salsa, whose bright, varied flavors are a nice counterpoint to the sweeter, more delicate fish (look for domestic tilapia for a sustainable seafood choice). If you have leftovers, serve the salsa on top of slices of toasted bread as gazpacho bruschetta. • **Serves 6**

4½ teaspoons sherry vinegar or red wine vinegar, or more to taste
 2 cloves garlic, pressed through a garlic press or minced
1½ teaspoons smoked paprika (see note on page 73)
 2 teaspoons coarse kosher salt, divided, or more to taste
 ½ teaspoon freshly ground black pepper, divided, or more to taste
 7 tablespoons extra virgin olive oil, divided
 1 large tomato, cored, seeded, and cut into ¼-inch dice
 ½ small cucumber, peeled and cut into ¼-inch dice
 ½ yellow bell pepper, cored, seeded, and cut into ¼-inch dice
 ¼ cup chopped red onion
 ⅓ cup pitted good-quality black olives, coarsely chopped
 2 tablespoons chopped fresh flat-leaf parsley
   Six 6-ounce tilapia fillets, about ¾ inch thick

■ In a small bowl, combine the vinegar, garlic, paprika, 1 teaspoon of the salt, and ¼ teaspoon of the black pepper, whisking to dissolve the salt. Whisk in 3 tablespoons of the olive oil. Set aside. (You can prepare the dressing up to 3 days in advance, storing it covered in the refrigerator.)

■ In a medium bowl, combine the tomato, cucumber, bell pepper, onion, olives, and parsley. Add the dressing and toss gently. Taste, ideally with your wine, and add more vinegar, salt, and/or black pepper if you like. (You can prepare the salsa up to a day in advance, storing it covered in the refrigerator.)

■ In each of two large nonstick skillets over medium-high heat, warm 2 tablespoons of the remaining olive oil. Sprinkle the fish with the remaining 1 teaspoon of salt and remaining ¼ teaspoon of black pepper. Add 3 fillets to each skillet and cook until well browned and cooked through, 2 to 3 minutes per side. (If you don't have two large nonstick skillets, cook the fish in batches.)

■ Serve the fish hot, with the salsa on top.

FOOD + WINE TIP If your Rosé is very dry and your tomatoes are very sweet, you might notice your wine tastes a bit sour. Simply sprinkle a little salt over your food, or drizzle it with a little lemon juice or vinegar, and things should come into balance.

marinated chicken with lavender and arugula

I was having a pool party and wanted to serve a dish that would be easy to throw on the grill, but that would make my guests feel like they had been treated to something special. Coincidentally, I noticed the arugula in my garden was growing rather wildly out of control. Severe snipping inspired this recipe, a simple—yet tasty—enhancement of plain old grilled chicken breasts.

Note that the chicken needs to marinate for four to twelve hours before grilling. • **Serves 4**

      2 ounces Parmesan cheese
     ¼ cup balsamic vinegar
     ¼ cup red wine vinegar
      1 tablespoon honey
      2 teaspoons dried lavender flowers (see note on page 134)
      2 teaspoons chopped fresh rosemary
    2½ teaspoons coarse kosher salt, divided
      1 teaspoon freshly ground black pepper, divided
      6 tablespoons extra virgin olive oil
      4 large boneless chicken breasts (1¾ to 2 pounds), ideally skin-on
      6 cups loosely packed arugula (about 3 ounces)

■ Use a vegetable peeler to cut the cheese into thick shaves (you should have about ⅔ cup). (You can shave the cheese up to a day in advance, storing it covered in the refrigerator.)

■ In a medium bowl, combine the vinegars, honey, lavender, rosemary, 1 teaspoon of the salt, and ½ teaspoon of the pepper, whisking to dissolve the salt. Whisk in the olive oil. Set 2 tablespoons of the mixture aside. Place the chicken in a large resealable bag, add the remaining olive oil mixture, and seal, squeezing out as much air as possible. Set aside in the refrigerator for 4 to 12 hours, turning occasionally.

■ Prepare the grill to medium-high heat and lightly oil the grate. Remove the chicken from the marinade and pat it dry (discard the marinade). Sprinkle the chicken with the remaining 1½ teaspoons of salt and remaining ½ teaspoon of pepper. Grill the chicken until it's cooked through, 3 or 4 minutes per side. Transfer to a platter and let it rest, loosely covered with foil, for 5 minutes.

■ Meanwhile, in a large bowl, combine the arugula with the reserved olive oil mixture, tossing to combine.

■ Arrange the arugula on a platter or plates and top with the chicken. Sprinkle with the shaved cheese and serve.

steak soft tacos with cilantro slaw and chipotle cream

Chipotle pepper adds a wonderfully smoldering heat to these tacos. Look for chipotles in the ethnic or Latin section of most major supermarkets. • **Serves 6**

1 cup sour cream
½ chipotle pepper from a can of chipotle peppers in adobo sauce, seeded and finely minced
2¼ teaspoons coarse kosher salt, divided
3 or 4 limes
¼ teaspoon freshly ground black pepper
2 tablespoons canola, grapeseed, or other neutral-flavored oil
One 10-ounce bag finely shredded cabbage or slaw mix (about 8 cups)
1 cup coarsely chopped fresh cilantro
1¼ to 1½ pounds boneless sirloin steak or flank steak, about ¾ inch thick
2 teaspoons smoked paprika (see note on page 73)
1½ teaspoons chili powder
1 teaspoon granulated garlic powder
1 teaspoon granulated onion powder
Twelve 6- or 8-inch corn or flour tortillas

■ In a small bowl, combine the sour cream, chipotle, and ¼ teaspoon of the salt, whisking to dissolve the salt. Set aside. (You can prepare the chipotle cream up to 3 days in advance, storing it covered in the refrigerator.)

■ Halve and squeeze 1 or 2 of the limes to yield 2 tablespoons of juice. In another small bowl, combine the lime juice, black pepper, and ½ teaspoon of the remaining salt, whisking to dissolve the salt. Whisk in the oil. In a large bowl, combine the cabbage and cilantro. Add the dressing mixture to the cabbage mixture, tossing to combine. Set aside. Cut the remaining 2 limes into 6 wedges each. Set aside. (You can prepare the cilantro slaw and lime wedges up to a day in advance, storing them covered in the refrigerator.)

■ Prepare the grill to high heat and lightly oil the grate. Sprinkle the steak with the paprika, chili powder, garlic powder, onion powder, and remaining 1½ teaspoons of salt. Wrap the tortillas in foil. Grill the steak to desired doneness, about 4 minutes per side for medium rare. Place the tortillas on a cooler part of the grill and cook until warm, 5 to 8 minutes, turning halfway through. Remove the steak from the grill and let it rest, loosely covered with foil, for 5 minutes.

■ Cut the steak across the grain diagonally into thin slices. Divide among the tortillas and top with the cilantro slaw and a dollop of the chipotle cream. Serve warm, with the lime wedges on the side.

pinot noir

erhaps not surprisingly, friends and family sometimes give my husband and me bottles of wine for gifts or to mark special occasions. And while we completely enjoy all kinds of wine, certain types tend to linger longer in our collection. But Pinot Noir—it's gone pretty quickly.

It's simply because, in our everyday life, we tend to eat fewer and fewer of the heavier foods that merit heavier red wines. And, increasingly, we enjoy the relatively lighter foods that pair with Pinot Noir. Pinot is just a great bridge wine, falling in between the crispness of a white and the intensity of a big, bold red—and making it perfect for all the foods that are similarly in the middle of the spectrum.

pinot noir by another name

• **Burgundy, Red Burgundy.** As with other French wines, these French Pinot Noirs are labeled with the name of the area they're from. They might have the general area name Burgundy, or names of subregions within Burgundy (Côte d'Or, for example). Basically, any red wine from Burgundy, with the exception of those from Beaujolais, will be made from the Pinot Noir grape.

pairing with pinot noir

Although there are, of course, nuances to Pinot Noir, the most important factors in food and wine pairing aren't a wine's nuances, but its broad strokes. If you learn a wine's overall characteristics and combine that information with the General Pairing Tips (page 8), you'll have a near-perfect pairing every time.

Broad characteristics:
• dry (not sweet)
• medium in acidity, crispness, or brightness
• medium-low to medium in tannins
• medium weight
• medium intensity

Pairs well with dishes that are:
• not sweet
• medium in acidity, crispness, or brightness
• medium-low to medium in richness/meatiness/heaviness, acidity, or slight bitterness
• medium weight
• medium intensity

For example, grilled salmon, turkey with gravy, or roast mush-rooms.

Another way to think of Pinot Noir is, pair it with foods that are too meaty for a white wine, but too light for a bigger red wine.

fine-tuning

Pinot Noir can be very earthy, so it never hurts to add some earthy element to the food you'll be enjoying with it. Mushrooms, cured olives, woody herbs like rosemary or thyme, and earthy spices like paprika, fennel, and cumin—all of these will help.

Pinot can also have lots of red berry flavors—raspberries, straw-berries, and cranberries. Adding any of these, especially raspberries and cranberries since they're not sweet, can improve Pinot pairings.

And as with other wines, acid and salt continue to be important. To complement Pinot Noir, think red wine vinegar, sherry vinegar, and if the rest of the dish is bright enough, even balsamic vinegar.

other nuances

Once you have a pairing that's working on the basis of sweetness, acidity, tannins, weight, and intensity, you can start playing with subtler nuances.

In addition to the earthiness and red berries mentioned above, some of the subtle flavors that you might find in a Pinot Noir include blackberries, cherries, pomegranate, herbs, and licorice. So it works to add those flavors, or foods that complement them, to your dishes.

other thoughts

Some foods that are considered classic pairings with Pinot Noir are salmon, tuna, mushrooms and mushroom sauces, poultry (espe-cially duck), lamb, veal, pork, and beef (especially lean and/or rare).

portobello mushroom sandwiches with brie and oregano aïoli

The mushrooms, Brie, oregano, and even the whole wheat buns all echo the earthy qualities in the wine. • **Serves 4**

⅓ cup mayonnaise
1 tablespoon chopped fresh oregano
2 teaspoons Dijon mustard
2 cloves garlic, pressed through a garlic press or minced
1¼ teaspoons coarse kosher salt, divided
¾ teaspoon freshly ground black pepper, divided
4 portobello mushrooms, stems trimmed
¼ cup extra virgin olive oil
4 ounces Brie cheese, cut into ¼-inch-thick slices
4 whole wheat buns, split horizontally
3 cups loosely packed arugula (about 1½ ounces)

■ In a small bowl, combine the mayonnaise, oregano, mustard, garlic, ¼ teaspoon of the salt, and ¼ teaspoon of the pepper. Set aside. (You can prepare the aïoli up to 4 hours in advance, storing it covered in the refrigerator.)

■ Prepare the grill to medium-high heat. Brush the mushrooms with the olive oil and sprinkle with the remaining 1 teaspoon of salt and remaining ½ teaspoon of pepper. Grill the mushrooms until tender and lightly charred, 4 to 5 minutes per side. During the last minute, arrange the cheese on top of the gill side of the mushrooms, dividing it evenly, and place the buns on the grill, cut side down, to melt the cheese and lightly toast the buns.

■ Place the mushrooms on the bottom halves of the buns. Top with the aïoli, arugula, and bun tops and serve hot.

red wine = tannins

Tannins are the compounds that give you that dry-mouth sensation in a red wine, usually with some bitterness. Tannins occur naturally in the skin of all grapes. But in most white wine making, the juice is fermented without the skins and so it doesn't pick up the tannins. (Tannins also come from oak aging, so some white wines do have a few.)

Good tannins help give a wine ageability, structure, and interest. And they soften over time. So they're not bad, but they do have to be taken into account.

So, per General Pairing Tip 3 (page 8), the red wine chapters' recipes use more rich/meaty/heavy and bitter elements. Per General Pairing Tip 5 (page 9), the food will also be more intense. And just as acid and salt have helped to balance acid in wine, per Fine-Tuning Tip 1 (page 9), they'll be important to balance tannins, too.

summer garden galette

In the late summer, when your garden or the farmer's market is brimming with full-flavored produce, this rustic tart is a great way to celebrate the bounty. • **Serves 6 to 8**

1 onion
1 large red bell pepper, quartered, cored, and seeded
3 tablespoons extra virgin olive oil, divided
2½ teaspoons coarse kosher salt, divided
1¼ teaspoons freshly ground black pepper, divided
    Four ½-inch-thick crosswise slices globe eggplant (about half of a 1-pound eggplant)
    Pastry dough for one 11-inch tart or 9-inch deep-dish pie, homemade or store-bought
6 ounces Gruyère cheese, shredded (you should have about 2⅓ cups), divided
2 tomatoes (about 12 ounces), cored and cut into ½-inch slices
1 tablespoon chopped fresh thyme

▓ Keeping the root end intact, cut the onion into 12 wedges.

▓ Prepare the grill to medium-high heat. In a large bowl, toss the onion, bell pepper, 1 tablespoon of the olive oil, 1½ teaspoons of the salt, and ¾ teaspoon of the black pepper. Brush the eggplant with the remaining 2 tablespoons of olive oil and sprinkle with ½ teaspoon of the remaining salt and ¼ teaspoon of the remaining black pepper. Grill the onions and bell pepper until softened and lightly charred, 4 to 5 minutes per side. Grill the eggplant until tender and lightly charred, about 3 minutes per side. Set aside to cool.

▓ Trim the roots off of the onion pieces, cut the bell peppers into ¼-inch strips, and cut the eggplant into ½-inch strips. Set aside. (You can prepare the onions, bell pepper, and eggplant up to 3 days in advance, storing them covered in the refrigerator. Return them to room temperature before proceeding.)

▓ Preheat the oven to 400°F. Line a rimmed baking sheet with parchment.

▓ On a lightly floured surface, roll out the dough to a 14-inch circle. Transfer the dough to the prepared baking sheet. Sprinkle 1⅔ cups of the cheese on the dough, leaving a 2-inch border. Arrange the tomato slices on top and sprinkle with the remaining ½ teaspoon of salt and remaining ¼ teaspoon of black pepper. Arrange the onions, bell pepper, and eggplant on top, then sprinkle with the thyme and remaining ⅔ cup of cheese. Carefully fold the dough border up and over the edge of the fillings, pinching it together every inch or two, forming a rustic crust. Bake until the crust is golden and the cheese is bubbly, about 45 minutes. Let the galette cool for 10 minutes before slicing and serving hot.

grilled salmon with rosemary pesto

This recipe makes about twice as much pesto as you'll need, but it's virtually impossible to make less because the amount would be too small for the food processor to puree. But that's a good thing, because you can use the extra the next time you grill salmon—or chicken, or another fish. It's also great on a grilled sausage sandwich.

For a sustainable seafood option, look for domestic, wild-caught salmon. • **Serves 4**

    1   cup loosely packed fresh flat-leaf parsley leaves
    ½   cup grated Asiago cheese (2½ to 3 ounces)
    ¼   cup loosely packed fresh rosemary leaves
    ¼   cup coarsely chopped walnuts, toasted (see note on page 18)
    2   cloves garlic
    1½ teaspoons coarse kosher salt, divided
    1   teaspoon freshly ground black pepper, divided
    7   tablespoons extra virgin olive oil, divided
        Four 6-ounce salmon fillets, about ¾ inch thick, skin removed if you like

▧ In the bowl of a food processor, combine the parsley, cheese, rosemary, walnuts, garlic, ½ teaspoon of the salt, and ½ teaspoon of the pepper and process to finely chop, scraping down the bowl as necessary. With the motor running, slowly add 5 tablespoons of the olive oil and process until smooth, scraping down the bowl as necessary. (You can prepare the pesto in advance, storing it covered in the refrigerator for up to a week or in the freezer for several months. To keep refrigerated pesto nicely green, cover it with a thin layer of olive oil—or simply restir it before serving.)

▧ Prepare the grill to medium-high heat. Brush the salmon with the remaining 2 tablespoons of olive oil and sprinkle with the remaining 1 teaspoon of salt and remaining ½ teaspoon of pepper. Grill the fish until cooked through, about 4 minutes per side.

▧ Serve the salmon hot, with about half of the pesto draped on top (save the remaining pesto for another use).

FOOD + WINE TIP Red wine with fish? Absolutely. In fact, salmon and Pinot Noir, in almost any incarnation, is considered one of the all-time great food and wine pairings.

warm duck and raspberry salad

Roast duck, bold greens, a bright vinaigrette, and sweet-tart berries—
a plateful of perfection, if you ask me. • **Serves 6**

6 boneless, skin-on duck breasts (2½ to 3 pounds)
6 shallots, thinly sliced
1 tablespoon chopped fresh rosemary
1 teaspoon coarse kosher salt, divided
½ teaspoon freshly ground black pepper, divided
10 teaspoons red wine vinegar, divided
1 small head radicchio, halved, cored, and cut into ¼-inch shreds (you should
  have about 3½ cups)
6 cups loosely packed arugula (about 3 ounces)
½ cup raspberries
¾ teaspoon coarse fleur de sel, other coarse finishing salt, or coarse kosher salt

▓ Preheat the oven to 350°F.

▓ Arrange the duck, skin side up, on a rimmed baking sheet and
bake until an internal thermometer reads 140°F for medium rare, 20
to 25 minutes. Transfer to a cutting board and let it rest, uncovered,
until cool enough to handle, about 10 minutes (leave the oven on if
preparing the duck on the day you're serving it). (You can prepare the
duck up to 3 days in advance, storing it covered in the refrigerator.
Return it to room temperature before serving.)

▓ Remove the skin from the duck, return the skin to the baking
sheet, and bake until very crisp, about 30 minutes. Set aside until
cool enough to handle, about 10 minutes. Reserve 3 tablespoons of
duck fat from the baking sheet (discard the remaining fat or save it for
another use).

▓ Meanwhile, in a small skillet over medium heat, warm 2 tablespoons of the duck fat. Add the shallots, rosemary, ½ teaspoon of
the coarse kosher salt, and ¼ teaspoon of the pepper and cook until
the shallots are softened, about 4 minutes. Remove from the heat
and gently stir in 5 teaspoons of the vinegar. Set aside.

▓ Cut the crisped duck skins into ¼-inch dice. Cut the duck breasts
on a diagonal into ½-inch slices (stir any accumulated juices into the
shallot mixture). Set aside.

▓ In a large bowl, combine the remaining 5 teaspoons of vinegar,
remaining 1 tablespoon of duck fat, remaining ½ teaspoon of coarse
kosher salt, and remaining ¼ teaspoon of pepper, whisking to dissolve the salt. Add the radicchio and arugula and toss to combine.

▓ Arrange the salad on a platter or plates. Arrange the duck breasts
and shallot mixture on top, dividing them evenly. Sprinkle with the
raspberries, crisped duck skins, and coarse fleur de sel and serve.

pork loin roast with dried cranberry stuffing

This beautiful roast would make a great holiday or other special-occasion entrée, the spiral of magenta stuffing giving it a decidedly festive flair.

Since the recipe features dried cranberries, it would make sense for the juice in the recipe to be cranberry as well. But 100 percent pomegranate juice is less sweet and so it works better with the wine.

- **Serves 8 to 10**

   4 thick slices bacon, cut crosswise into ¼-inch strips
   1 red onion, cut into ¼-inch dice
1½ cups 100 percent pomegranate juice, divided
   2 cups dried cranberries
     One 4-pound boneless pork loin, excess fat trimmed, ideally brined (see page 81)
 ½ cup panko (Japanese-style breadcrumbs)
   2 to 3 teaspoons coarse kosher salt, divided, plus more to taste
1½ teaspoons freshly ground black pepper, divided, plus more to taste
1½ teaspoons chopped fresh rosemary, divided
1½ teaspoons chopped fresh sage, divided
1½ teaspoons chopped fresh thyme, divided
   1 cup Pinot Noir, or other dry red wine
   2 tablespoons (¼ stick) unsalted butter, cut into 3 or 4 pieces
   1 tablespoon cornstarch dissolved in 1 tablespoon cold water

■ In a medium skillet over medium-low heat, cook the bacon, stirring occasionally, until crisp, about 10 minutes. Use a slotted spoon to transfer the bacon to a large bowl. Set aside to cool.

■ Increase the heat to medium-high. Add the onion to the skillet with the bacon fat and cook, stirring occasionally, until the onion is soft, about 3 minutes. Add ½ cup of the pomegranate juice and bring to a boil. Add the cranberries, remove from the heat, and set aside to plump the cranberries.

■ Meanwhile, place the pork on a cutting board, fat side down. With a very sharp boning or carving knife, cut down along one long side of the loin, about ½ inch from the edge and stopping ½ inch from the cutting board (this is the beginning of cutting the pork into a spiral). Turn your knife parallel to the cutting board and cut inward (parallel to the bottom of the roast), keeping the thickness of the meat as even as possible, using your other hand to gently lift the top portion of the meat away from the knife. Continue this cut until the loin is one long flat piece of meat, about ½ inch thick.

(continued on following page)

■ Add the cranberry mixture to the bowl with the bacon. Stir in the panko, 2 teaspoons of the salt, 1 teaspoon of the pepper, 1 teaspoon of the rosemary, 1 teaspoon of the sage, and 1 teaspoon of the thyme. Spread the stuffing evenly over the pork. Beginning at the end that was the interior, roll the roast back up and arrange it seam side down. Tie the roast with kitchen twine at 1- to 1½-inch intervals. Sprinkle on all sides with the remaining 1 teaspoon of salt (if you didn't brine) and remaining ½ teaspoon of pepper. (You can prepare the roast up to a day in advance, storing it covered in the refrigerator. Return it to room temperature before proceeding.)

■ Preheat the oven to 450°F.

■ Arrange the pork, fat side up, on a rack in a roasting pan large enough to comfortably hold it. Add about ¼ inch of water to the bottom of the pan and roast for 15 minutes.

■ Reduce the oven to 325°F and continue roasting until an internal thermometer inserted into the center of the meat reads 140°F, about 1 hour total cooking time. (If the pan gets dry, add more water to maintain about ¼ inch of liquid.) Transfer the pork to a cutting board and let it rest, loosely covered with foil, for 15 minutes. (It will continue to cook, reaching an internal temperature of about 150°F.)

■ Meanwhile, drain the roasting pan (discard the liquids). Place the pan on the stovetop over medium-high heat, straddled over two burners if necessary. Add the wine and remaining 1 cup of pomegranate juice, bring to a boil, and cook, scraping up any browned bits in the pan, until the liquid is reduced to 1 cup, about 8 minutes depending on the pan. Reduce to a simmer and add the butter, remaining ½ teaspoon of rosemary, remaining ½ teaspoon of sage, and remaining ½ teaspoon of thyme, stirring until the butter melts. Add the cornstarch mixture and cook until the sauce thickens, just a few seconds. Remove from the heat. Taste, ideally with your wine, and add salt (if you didn't brine) and/or pepper if you like.

■ Remove the twine and slice the pork crosswise, for a spiral of meat and stuffing. Drizzle with the pan sauce and serve hot.

 FOOD + WINE TIP If you don't brine, you might need to balance the sweetness of the cranberries with a sprinkle of salt at the table.

lamburgers with feta sauce and mint

A little Middle Eastern, a little all-American backyard barbecue, these burgers are hearty and refreshing at the same time. Serve them at your next cookout, with a bottle of Pinot Noir, for a delicious change of pace. • **Serves 4**

½ cup finely crumbled feta cheese (2½ to 3 ounces)
½ cup sour cream
2 tablespoons heavy whipping cream
1 tablespoon fresh lemon juice
1 teaspoon prepared horseradish
2¼ teaspoons coarse kosher salt, divided
1¾ teaspoons freshly ground black pepper, divided
1¼ pounds ground lamb
¼ cup chopped fresh flat-leaf parsley
1 large shallot, finely diced
2 cloves garlic, pressed through a garlic press or minced
1 cup loosely packed fresh mint leaves
1 cup loosely packed mixed salad greens (about ½ ounce)
2 rounds whole wheat pita bread, cut in half to make 4 pita pockets

▦ In a small bowl, combine the cheese, sour cream, cream, lemon juice, horseradish, ¼ teaspoon of the salt, and ¾ teaspoon of the pepper. Set aside. (You can prepare the feta sauce up to 2 days in advance, storing it covered in the refrigerator. Return it to room temperature before serving.)

▦ In a large bowl, combine the lamb, parsley, shallot, garlic, remaining 2 teaspoons of salt, and remaining 1 teaspoon of pepper and gently mix well. With dampened hands, shape the mixture into 4 oblong patties, about 4 inches long and ¾ inch thick. (You can shape the patties up to 2 days in advance, storing them covered in the refrigerator.)

▦ In a medium bowl, combine the mint and salad greens. Set aside.

▦ Prepare the grill to medium-high heat and lightly oil the grate. Grill the patties to desired doneness, about 3½ minutes per side for medium. During the last minute, place the pitas on the grill and turn to lightly toast both sides.

▦ To serve, place a lamburger in each pita pocket. Add the mint mixture and feta sauce, dividing them evenly, and serve hot.

cumin and smoked paprika leg of lamb

You might think leg of lamb something fancy and complicated, but really, it's just a roast. Flavor it with a little something, put it in the oven, and—ta da!—a delicious, hearty meal with relatively little fuss.

This particular preparation is the opposite of highbrow. The spices impart earthy, rustic notes that pair beautifully with typically earthy Pinot Noir. On the side, try roasted carrots or cauliflower, or garlic mashed potatoes. • **Serves 6 to 8**

¼ cup cumin seeds, toasted (see note on page 49)
¼ cup extra virgin olive oil
2 tablespoons smoked paprika (see note on page 73)
1 tablespoon coarse kosher salt, or more to taste
1 tablespoon fresh lemon juice
¼ teaspoon cayenne pepper
1 semiboneless leg of lamb (5 to 5½ pounds), excess fat trimmed

▨ Use a mortar and pestle to lightly crush the cumin seeds. (If you don't have a mortar and pestle, place them in a small bowl and lightly crush them with the end of a wooden spoon.) Stir in the olive oil, paprika, salt, lemon juice, and cayenne. Set aside. (You can prepare the rub up to 3 days in advance, storing it covered in the refrigerator.)

▨ Preheat the oven to 450°F.

▨ Arrange the lamb fat side down on a rack in a roasting pan large enough to comfortably hold it. Pour about one-third of the olive oil mixture on top, rubbing it all over the meat. Turn the lamb fat side up and repeat with the remaining two-thirds of the olive oil mixture. Add about ¼ inch of water to the bottom of the pan and roast for 20 minutes.

▨ Reduce the oven to 350°F and baste the lamb with the pan juices. Continue roasting, basting every 15 or 20 minutes, until an internal thermometer inserted into the center of the meat without touching the bone reads 130°F for medium rare, about 1 hour and 20 minutes total cooking time. (If the pan gets dry, pour in more water to maintain about ¼ inch of liquid.) Transfer the lamb to a cutting board and let it rest, loosely covered with foil, for 15 minutes. (It will continue to cook, reaching an internal temperature of about 140°F.)

▨ Taste the pan juices, ideally with your wine, and add more salt if you like. Carve the lamb and serve it hot, with the pan juices spooned on top.

merlot

love Merlot. There, I said it.

Why is it risky to admit liking Merlot? Well, like Chardonnay, many think that if it's that popular, there must be something wrong with it. You could also argue that the wine's huge popularity has led to a glut of plonk Merlot. And you can even blame "the *Sideways* effect," thanks to the anti-Merlot rant of a character in the movie.

But the fact remains that lush, fruity Merlot is a great food wine. It can be big and rich, but also fruity and soft, without being overly high in acids or tannins that you have to work around.

So, if you've been a Merlot lover all along, good for you. And if not, take a risk.

merlot by another name

• **Bordeaux, Red Bordeaux.** As with other French wines, these French Merlot blends are labeled with the name of the area they're from. They might have the general name Bordeaux, or the names of subregions within Bordeaux (Pomerol, for example). In blends from the Left Bank of Bordeaux, Cabernet will be the dominant grape, followed by Merlot. On the Right Bank, Merlot dominates. • **Meritage.** A group of American vintners have trademarked this name, pronounced to rhyme with "heritage," for Bordeaux-style blends made in the United States. These wines often include Merlot but may or may not be mostly Merlot.

pairing with merlot

Although there are, of course, nuances to Merlot, the most important factors in food and wine pairing aren't a wine's nuances, but its broad strokes. If you learn a wine's overall characteristics and combine that information with the General Pairing Tips (page 8), you'll have a near-perfect pairing every time.

Broad characteristics:
- dry (not sweet)
- medium in acidity, crispness, or brightness
- medium in tannins
- medium to heavy weight
- medium to strong intensity

Pairs well with dishes that are:

- not sweet
- medium in acidity, crispness, or brightness
- medium in richness/meatiness/heaviness, acidity, or slight bitterness
- medium to heavy weight
- medium to strong intensity

For example, duck with plum sauce, lamb stew, or mushroom risotto.

fine-tuning

As always, salt and acid are important. But because Merlot is generally a soft wine, you won't need as much of them. Should you decide on a dash of something acidic, try balsamic vinegar. It beautifully mirrors the dark berry flavors in the wine.

Speaking of dark berries, because Merlot is a fruity wine, it can pair well with foods that have a fruity element, especially dark fruits like blackberries and black cherries. But remember that fruit can add sweetness, making your wine taste sour. So use tart fruits, balance the sweetness with acid, or add fruitiness without adding sweetness—by using fruit zest, fruit-infused vinegars and oils, or even dried fruits, which tend to be less sweet than their fresh counterparts.

other nuances

Once you have a pairing that's working on the basis of sweetness, acidity, tannins, weight, and intensity, you can start playing with subtler nuances.

In addition to the fruitiness mentioned above—especially plums, cherries, and dark berries like blackberries, boysenberries, and black currants—some of the subtle flavors that you might find in a Merlot include green pepper, baking spices, chocolate, cedar, and herbs. So it works to add those flavors, or foods that complement them, to your dishes.

other thoughts

Some foods that are considered classic pairings with Merlot are duck and other gamier poultry, lamb, pork loin, mushrooms, beef (especially roast beef and filet mignon), and blue, fruity, and nutty cheeses.

eggplant moussaka

Although moussaka is Greek in origin, it has a decidedly Middle Eastern, and even Moroccan, flair, with baking spices like cinnamon and nutmeg interwoven with savory ingredients including eggplant, potatoes, tomatoes, and mushrooms. All combined, it's a hearty, satisfying vegetarian option the whole table will enjoy.

Don't be intimidated by the long list of ingredients—you probably have most of them on hand. • **Serves 8**

½ cup extra virgin olive oil, divided, plus more for the baking sheets and baking pan
3 large russet potatoes (about 2¾ pounds), cut into ¼-inch slices
2 large globe eggplants (about 3 pounds), cut into ½-inch slices
1 large carrot, cut into ¼-inch dice
1 large onion, cut into ¼-inch dice
12 ounces portobello mushrooms, cut into ¼-inch dice (you should have about 5 cups)
4 cloves garlic, thinly sliced
One 28-ounce can crushed tomatoes
½ cup dried currants
⅓ cup Merlot, or other dry red wine
4 teaspoons balsamic vinegar
1 teaspoon soy sauce
¼ teaspoon ground cinnamon
3½ teaspoons coarse kosher salt, divided, or more to taste
⅝ teaspoon freshly ground black pepper, divided, or more to taste
⅜ teaspoon ground nutmeg, preferably freshly grated, divided
1 cup shredded extra-sharp Cheddar cheese (about 4 ounces), divided
4 large egg yolks
6 tablespoons (¾ stick) unsalted butter
6 tablespoons all-purpose flour
3¼ cups milk (low-fat is okay)

■ Preheat the oven to 425°F. Arrange one rack in the bottom quarter of the oven, one in the middle, and another in the top quarter.

■ Coat three rimmed baking sheets with olive oil. Arrange the potato and eggplant slices in a single layer on the sheets (you may not be able to fit all the slices—save any remaining slices for another use) and brush with 6 tablespoons of the olive oil. Bake until tender, about 20 minutes, turning halfway through. Set aside to cool.

■ While the potato and eggplant are cooking, in a large skillet over medium heat, warm the remaining 2 tablespoons of olive oil. Add the carrot and cook, stirring occasionally, for 2 minutes. Add the onion and cook, stirring occasionally, until the carrot and onion are tender, about 6 minutes. Add the mushrooms and garlic and cook, stirring occasionally, until the mushrooms are tender, about 5 minutes. Stir in the tomatoes, currants, wine, vinegar, soy sauce, cinnamon, 1½ teaspoons of the salt, ½ teaspoon of the pepper, and ¼ teaspoon of the nutmeg. Bring to a boil, reduce to a simmer, and cook, stirring occasionally, until the mixture thickens, 10 to 12 minutes. Taste, ideally with your wine, and add more salt and/or pepper if you like. (You can prepare the potatoes, eggplant, and tomato mixture up to 3 days in advance, storing them covered in the refrigerator. Return them to room temperature before proceeding if you'll be assembling the moussaka on the day you'll be cooking it.)

■ Reduce the oven to 350°F. Lightly oil a 9 x 13-inch baking pan.

■ Arrange half of the potato in a single layer in the pan, cutting the slices to fit. Arrange half of the eggplant in a single layer on top, cutting the slices to fit, and sprinkle with ¾ teaspoon of the remaining salt. Spoon half of the tomato mixture over the eggplant and sprinkle with 2 tablespoons of the cheese. Repeat with the remaining potato, remaining eggplant, ¾ teaspoon of the remaining salt, the remaining tomato mixture, and 2 tablespoons of the remaining cheese (you may not need all the potato and eggplant). Set aside.

■ Place the egg yolks in a medium bowl. Set aside.

■ In a medium saucepan over medium heat, melt the butter. Sprinkle in the flour and, whisking constantly, cook for 2 minutes. Slowly add the milk, whisking out any lumps of flour, and cook, stirring occasionally, until the sauce thickens and comes to a simmer, 5 to 7 minutes. Remove from the heat and stir in ½ cup of the remaining cheese, the remaining ½ teaspoon of salt, remaining ⅛ teaspoon of pepper, and remaining ⅛ teaspoon of nutmeg. Stir about ½ cup of the sauce into the egg yolks, then add the egg yolk mixture back into the sauce, gently stirring until the eggs are combined. Pour the sauce over the baking pan. Sprinkle with the remaining ¼ cup of cheese. (You can prepare the moussaka up to a day in advance, storing it covered in the refrigerator. Return it to room temperature before proceeding.)

■ Place the moussaka on a rimmed baking sheet and bake until heated through and golden brown on top, 50 to 60 minutes. Cool 15 minutes before serving.

FOOD + WINE TIP Key to this pairing is heavying up on the tomatoes, along with adding a dash of vinegar, for brightness. Also, using Cheddar cheese instead of the more traditional Parmesan adds a creaminess that complements rich Merlot.

mixed mushroom pappardelle

I like big, meaty pappardelle with this rich mushroom sauce. But if you can't find it, you can substitute fusilli, farfalle, rigatoni, or another favorite shape. • **Serves 4**

12 ounces pappardelle pasta
2 tablespoons extra virgin olive oil
1 pound mixed meaty mushrooms, such as white, brown, cremini, baby portobello, or shiitake, cut into ¼-inch slices, stems removed from shiitakes (you should have about 7 cups)
4 cloves garlic, thinly sliced
½ cup Merlot, or other dry red wine
1 tablespoon chopped fresh thyme, plus sprigs for garnish
1 cup crème fraîche
1 cup reduced-sodium chicken or vegetable broth
1½ teaspoons coarse kosher salt, or more to taste
¾ teaspoon freshly ground black pepper, or more to taste
1 teaspoon soy sauce
1 to 2 tablespoons balsamic vinegar, ideally good-quality aged balsamic

■ In a large pot of boiling, well-salted water (1 tablespoon of coarse kosher salt per quart), cook the pasta according to package directions.

■ Meanwhile, in a large skillet over medium-high heat, warm the olive oil. Add the mushrooms and cook, stirring occasionally, for 3 minutes. Add the garlic and cook, stirring occasionally, until the mushrooms are almost tender, about 2 minutes. Add the wine and chopped thyme and cook, scraping up any browned bits on the bottom of the skillet, until the liquid has almost entirely evaporated, 1 to 2 minutes. Reduce to a simmer, add the crème fraîche, and stir until incorporated. Stir in the broth, salt, pepper, and soy sauce. Taste, ideally with your wine, and add more salt and/or pepper to taste.

■ Drain the pasta, immediately add it to the skillet, and toss to coat. Serve the pasta hot, drizzled with the vinegar and garnished with the thyme sprigs. (You can also pass a bottle of balsamic vinegar at the table.)

FOOD + WINE TIP You may have noticed that a lot of the recipes in this chapter include balsamic vinegar. It's just a great tool when pairing with Merlot—adding acidity, yes, but also adding dark berry fruit flavors that perfectly complement the wine.

duck breasts with wild rice, pecans, and pomegranate

If you can pan-sear a steak or a chicken breast, you can cook a duck breast. There is a little secret, however, to getting rid of most of that fat right below the skin. What you do is score the breasts, and then sear them, skin side down, rendering out the fat. After that, juicy, tender meat is, well, duck soup! • **Serves 6**

 1 cup uncooked white and wild rice blend (see note on page 54)
 ½ cup chopped pecans, toasted (see note on page 18)
 10 tablespoons pomegranate arils, divided
 13 tablespoons 100% pomegranate juice, divided
 2 teaspoons coarse kosher salt, divided
 1¼ teaspoons freshly ground black pepper, divided
 6 boneless, skin-on duck breasts (2½ to 3 pounds)
 4½ teaspoons balsamic vinegar

■ Cook the rice according to package directions. Remove from the heat and stir in the pecans, ½ cup of the pomegranate arils, 1 tablespoon of the pomegranate juice, ½ teaspoon of the salt, and ¼ teaspoon of the pepper. Cover and set aside.

■ While the rice is cooking, trim any silver skin from the meaty side of the duck breasts. If the tender is still attached, scrape the tendon out and pat the tender back in place. Trim the skin to no more than ¼-inch overhang. Use a sharp knife to score the skin in a crosshatch pattern, with the cuts about ½ inch apart, being careful not to cut into the meat. Sprinkle both sides of the duck with the remaining 1½ teaspoons of salt and remaining 1 teaspoon of pepper.

■ Heat two large skillets over medium-high heat. Add the duck, skin side down, and cook until medium brown, about 6 minutes. As the fat renders, spoon it off once or twice. Reduce the heat to medium and continue cooking until the skin is crisp and deeply golden brown, 2 to 4 minutes. Turn and cook until an internal thermometer reads 140°F for medium rare, 4 to 6 minutes. Transfer the duck to a cutting board and let it rest, loosely covered with foil, for 5 minutes.

■ Meanwhile, pour off the duck fat and return one of the skillets to medium-high heat (remove the other from the heat). Add the remaining ¾ cup of pomegranate juice, scrape up any browned bits on the bottom of the skillet, and cook until reduced to 6 tablespoons, about 3 minutes. Remove from the heat and stir in the vinegar.

■ Cut the duck on a diagonal into ½-inch slices. Arrange the rice on a platter or plates, top with the duck, and drizzle with the pan sauce, along with any accumulated juices. Sprinkle with the remaining 2 tablespoons of pomegranate arils and serve hot.

skillet-roasted chicken breasts with lavender and red wine–butter sauce

This beautiful dish has a decidedly feminine flair, with a silky pink sauce and a flower garnish. But don't let that prevent you from serving it to the most manly of men—it's amazingly seductive. • **Serves 4**

- 2 tablespoons extra virgin olive oil
- 4 large boneless chicken breasts (1¾ to 2 pounds), ideally skin-on
- ½ teaspoon freshly ground black pepper
- 1¾ teaspoons coarse kosher salt, divided, or more to taste
- ⅓ cup heavy whipping cream
- ⅓ cup Merlot, or other dry red wine
- 1 shallot, finely diced
- ½ teaspoon red wine vinegar
- ½ teaspoon dried lavender flowers (see below)
- 6 tablespoons (¾ stick) unsalted butter, cut into 6 or 8 pieces
- ¼ teaspoon white pepper, ideally freshly ground, or more to taste
  Fresh lavender sprigs, for garnish (optional)

■ Preheat the oven to 450°F.

■ In a large ovenproof skillet over medium-high heat, warm the olive oil. Sprinkle the chicken on both sides with the black pepper and 1 teaspoon of the salt. Cook the chicken, skin side down, until browned, about 5 minutes. Turn the chicken, place the skillet in the oven, and roast until the chicken is cooked through, 8 to 10 minutes. Transfer the chicken to a platter or plates (be careful—the handle of the skillet will be very hot) and let it rest, loosely covered with foil, for 5 minutes.

■ While the chicken is in the oven, in a small saucepan over medium heat, combine the cream, wine, shallot, vinegar, and dried lavender and cook, stirring occasionally, until reduced to ⅓ cup, about 5 minutes. Remove from the heat and whisk in the butter, 2 or 3 pieces at a time, waiting until the pieces are melted before adding more. Stir in the white pepper and remaining ¾ teaspoon of salt. Taste, ideally with your wine, and add more salt and/or white pepper if you like. Cover to keep warm and set aside.

■ Serve the chicken hot, with the sauce drizzled on top, and garnished with the fresh lavender sprigs, if using.

NOTE Dried lavender flowers are available at specialty food stores and in the bulk dried herbs and flowers section at many natural food stores. Besides using them in this recipe, you can use them in Marinated Chicken with Lavender and Arugula (page 112), you can mix them into a dried herb blend called herbes de Provence (see note on page 52), and you can sprinkle them into baked goods and over roasting poultry.

chicken cocoa vin

Chopped unsweetened chocolate, stirred in at the end, gives this twist on coq au vin wonderful richness and adds subtle chocolate flavor without chocolate sweetness, which could cause the wine to taste sour.

Serving it over egg noodles adds another creamy element—but it would also be good sans noodles with a hunk of crusty bread on the side. • **Serves 4**

> One 6-ounce piece pancetta, cut into 1/2-inch dice (you should have
> about 1 1/2 cups) (see note on page 26)
> 1/3 cup all-purpose flour
> 1 teaspoon freshly ground black pepper, or more to taste
> 2 teaspoons coarse kosher salt, divided, or more to taste
> 4 large bone-in, skin-on chicken thighs (1 3/4 to 2 1/4 pounds)
> 3 carrots, cut into 1/4-inch slices
> 12 pearl or cipollini onions, trimmed, peeled, and halved
> 8 ounces brown or cremini mushrooms, halved or quartered if large
> 1 cup Merlot, or other dry red wine
> 4 cloves garlic, pressed through a garlic press or minced
> One 15-ounce can tomato sauce
> 6 ounces egg noodles
> 1 1/2 ounces good-quality unsweetened chocolate, coarsely chopped
> 2 tablespoons chopped fresh flat-leaf parsley

▨ In a large skillet over medium-low heat, cook the pancetta, stirring occasionally, until crisp, about 10 minutes. Use a slotted spoon to transfer the pancetta to a platter or plate. Set aside to cool.

▨ While the pancetta is cooking, in a large, shallow bowl, combine the flour, pepper, and 1 1/2 teaspoons of the salt. One piece at a time, dip the chicken in the flour mixture, shaking off the excess. Set the coated chicken on another platter or plate.

▨ Increase the heat under the skillet to medium-high, add the chicken, skin side down, and cook until browned, 3 to 4 minutes. Turn and brown the other side, 3 to 4 minutes. Transfer the chicken to the plate with the pancetta.

▨ Add the carrots and onions to the skillet and cook, stirring occasionally, for 2 minutes. Add the mushrooms and cook, stirring occasionally, until the vegetables are browned, 2 to 4 minutes. Add the wine, garlic, and remaining 1/2 teaspoon of salt and scrape up any browned bits on the bottom of the skillet. Stir in the tomato sauce. Nestle the chicken and pancetta back into the skillet and bring to a boil. Reduce to a simmer, cover, and cook until the chicken is cooked through, about 20 minutes.

■ Meanwhile, in a large pot of boiling, well-salted water (1 tablespoon of coarse kosher salt per quart), cook the noodles according to package directions.

■ Add the chocolate to the chicken mixture and stir until the chocolate melts. Taste the sauce, ideally with your wine, and add more salt and/or pepper if you like.

■ Drain the pasta and transfer it to a serving bowl or to individual bowls. Spoon the chicken and sauce on top. Sprinkle with the parsley and serve hot.

merlot + chocolate?

A lot of people think Merlot and chocolate—chocolate candy or eating chocolate—or Cabernet Sauvignon and chocolate, is a great combination, which would be an exception to General Pairing Tip 1 (page 8). I'm not one of them. Even though there are relatively few tannins, or there's little bitterness, in Merlot, the sweetness of chocolate nevertheless accentuates them and, to me, makes the wine taste terrible. And Cabernet, with even more tannins, is worse.

If you want to try to make this pairing work, your best bet is to use a really bittersweet chocolate—the less sugar and more bitterness in the chocolate, the less that accentuation of the wine's bitterness will happen. Or use unsweetened or baking chocolate, not on its own but as an ingredient a savory dish, like this recipe does.

merlot-braised lamb shanks with gorgonzola polenta

Slow cooking turns otherwise tough and sinewy shanks into unctu-
ous, falling-off-the-bone, to-die-for goodness—and you get a house
full of wonderful, warming smells in the process. Combined with the
gorgonzola-laced polenta and wine-y juices, this dish is as impressive
as it is mouthwatering. • **Serves 8**

 2 tablespoons chopped fresh rosemary
 2 tablespoons chopped fresh thyme
 4 teaspoons coarse kosher salt, divided, or more to taste
 3½ teaspoons freshly ground black pepper, divided, or more to taste
   Eight 1- to 1¼-pound lamb shanks
   About ¼ cup canola, grapeseed, or other neutral-flavored oil, divided
   Two 750-ml bottles Merlot, or other dry red wine
 2 tablespoons (¼ stick) unsalted butter, cut into 2 or 3 pieces
 2 teaspoons red wine vinegar
 5 to 6 cups reduced-sodium chicken broth
 1¾ cups polenta (see note on page 177)
   ¾ cup crumbled Gorgonzola cheese (about 3½ ounces)
   ⅓ cup heavy whipping cream

▓ In a small bowl, combine the rosemary, thyme, 1 tablespoon of the
salt, and 1 tablespoon of the pepper. Arrange the shanks in a dish or
pan large enough to hold them in a single layer and sprinkle the herb
mixture all over. Cover and refrigerate for 8 to 24 hours (see below).

▓ Preheat the oven to 375°F.

▓ In a roasting pan large enough to hold the shanks in a single layer,
over medium-high heat (on the stovetop), warm 2 tablespoons of the
oil. Add half of the shanks and cook until brown on all sides, about 8
minutes. Transfer to a large bowl or plate and repeat with the remaining shanks, adding more oil as needed.

▓ Pour off the oil in the pan, add the wine, and scrape up any
browned bits on the bottom. Return the shanks and any accumulated
juices to the pan, cover, and bake until the meat is very tender, 2 to
2½ hours, turning the shanks in the sauce halfway through. (You can
prepare the lamb shanks up to a day in advance, storing them covered in the refrigerator. Return to a simmer before proceeding.)

▓ Use tongs or a slotted spoon to transfer the shanks to a large bowl
or plate and cover to keep warm. Skim any fat from the top of the
braising liquid. Place the roasting pan on the stovetop over medium-
high heat, straddled over two burners if necessary, bring to a boil,
and cook until reduced to 2 cups, 20 to 25 minutes. Remove from
the heat and stir in the butter and vinegar.

■ While the liquid is reducing, in a large saucepan or small stockpot over high heat, bring 5 cups of the broth to a boil. Gradually add the polenta, whisking constantly. Return to a boil, reduce to a simmer, cover, and cook, stirring frequently and adding more broth by ¼ cupfuls if the polenta is too thick, until the polenta is tender, about 10 minutes. Remove from the heat and stir in the cheese, cream, remaining 1 teaspoon of salt, and remaining ½ teaspoon of pepper.

■ Arrange the polenta on plates, dividing it evenly. Top with the lamb shanks and sauce and serve hot.

NOTE It's not critical that the seasonings sit on the meat for the entire 8 to 24 hours, so don't let that prevent you from making the recipe. It does make a difference in both taste and texture, however, so **add the seasonings as far in advance as possible**, even if it's only 30 minutes.

FOOD + WINE TIP The general rule is you shouldn't cook with a wine that's so inexpensive you wouldn't drink it. But by the same token, you shouldn't use something too expensive. So opt for something in between, whatever that means for you.

bacon and blue cheese burgers

There's a reason this combination is ubiquitous on the menus of burger joints near and far, upscale and downtown. It's amazing.

Perhaps even more amazing, however, is how well it pairs with Merlot. Like the wine, this burger is rich. Plus, the bright, salty blue cheese brings out the fruit in the wine, while the bacon adds complementary meatiness. • **Serves 6**

    1½ cups crumbled blue cheese (about 6 ounces)
     6 tablespoons mayonnaise
     1 tablespoon Dijon mustard
    2½ teaspoons coarse kosher salt, divided
    1¼ teaspoons freshly ground black pepper, divided
    2½ pounds 80 percent lean ground beef
    12 thick slices bacon
     6 hamburger buns, split horizontally
     3 thin slices red onion, separated into rings

▓ In a medium bowl, combine the cheese, mayonnaise, mustard, ½ teaspoon of the salt, and ¼ teaspoon of the pepper. (You can prepare the cheese mixture in advance, storing it covered in the refrigerator for up to 3 days. Return it to room temperature before proceeding.)

▓ With dampened hands, shape the beef into 6 patties, about 4½ inches in diameter and ¾ inch thick. (You can shape the patties up to 2 days in advance, storing them covered in the refrigerator.)

▓ In a very large skillet over medium heat, cook 6 slices of the bacon until crisp and golden, 8 to 10 minutes, turning halfway through. Transfer the bacon to a paper towel–lined plate. Pour off the fat, wipe out the skillet, and repeat with the remaining 6 slices of bacon. Set aside.

▓ Prepare the grill to medium-high heat and lightly oil the grate. Sprinkle both sides of the patties with the remaining 2 teaspoons of salt and remaining 1 teaspoon of pepper. Grill to desired doneness, about 3 minutes per side for medium. During the last minute, place the buns on the grill, cut side down, to lightly toast.

▓ Place 2 slices of bacon on the bottom half of each bun. Top with the onion, patties, cheese mixture, and the top halves of the buns and serve.

baby beef wellingtons

Beef Wellington always feels elegant. And personally sized portions make it even more so.

On the side, continue the retro theme with creamed spinach or an iceberg wedge with blue cheese dressing. • **Serves 8**

2 sheets puff pastry (one 17.3-ounce package), thawed
Eight 6- to 7-ounce filet mignon medallions, about 1½ inches thick
3½ teaspoons coarse kosher salt, divided
1¼ teaspoons freshly ground black pepper, divided
3 tablespoons extra virgin olive oil, divided
8 shallots, cut into ¼-inch dice (you should have about 1½ cups)
8 cloves garlic, pressed through a garlic press or minced
2 ounces liver pâté (optional)
¼ cup Dijon mustard

▓ On a lightly floured surface, roll each sheet of the pastry out to a 12 x 12-inch square. Cut each sheet into 4 squares. Set the pastry squares aside in the refrigerator. (You can prepare the pastry up to 3 days in advance, storing it covered in the refrigerator.)

▓ Preheat the oven to 450°F (if you're planning to cook to medium rare and you have a convection setting, use it—if not, don't worry about it). Arrange one rack in the bottom third of the oven and another in the top third.

▓ Sprinkle the filets all over with 1 tablespoon of the salt and 1 teaspoon of the pepper.

▓ In each of two medium skillets over medium-high heat, warm 1 tablespoon of the olive oil. Add the filets and cook until well seared, about 2 minutes per side. Arrange the filets on two rimmed baking sheets and loosely cover with foil.

▓ Return one of the skillets to medium-high heat (remove the other from the heat) and add the remaining 1 tablespoon of olive oil. Add the shallots and cook, stirring occasionally, until tender, about 1 minute. Add the garlic and cook, stirring, until fragrant, about 1 minute. Stir in the remaining ½ teaspoon of salt and remaining ¼ teaspoon of pepper. Remove from the heat and set aside.

▓ Top each filet with some of the pâté, if using, dividing it evenly. Top with the mustard and the shallot mixture, dividing both evenly. Drape each filet with a square of the pastry, molding it over the top and down the sides of the meat, letting the corners fan out onto the baking sheet. Make 2 or 3 decorative slashes in the top of each pastry.

▓ Bake for 12 minutes for medium rare or 17 minutes for medium. Remove from the oven and let the filets rest, loosely covered with foil, for 10 minutes before serving hot.

zinfandel

infandel is a decidedly rootin' tootin' sort of wine. You could say it's as big as the Wild West and just as bold—with bright acid, juicy and often jammy fruit, sometimes-high alcohol levels, and even some spice.

A classic pairing with Zin? All-American barbecue.

Zinfandel also pairs beautifully with Italian foods, especially the tomato-based dishes of the south. And it works with mildly spicy foods, plus braised, grilled, and salty cured meats.

Generally speaking, if it's rich and robust, it'll work with Zinfandel. Yee hah!

zinfandel by another name
• **Primitivo.** This is the name for the same grape in Italy.

pairing with zinfandel
Although there are, of course, nuances to Zinfandel, the most important factors in food and wine pairing aren't a wine's nuances, but its broad strokes. If you learn a wine's overall characteristics and combine that information with the General Pairing Tips (page 8), you'll have a near-perfect pairing every time.

Broad characteristics:
• dry (not sweet)
• medium to high in acidity, crispness, or brightness
• medium to high in tannins
• medium to heavy weight
• medium to strong intensity

Pairs well with dishes that are:
• not sweet
• medium to high in acidity, crispness, or brightness
• medium to high in richness/meatiness/heaviness, acidity, or slight bitterness
• medium to heavy weight
• medium to strong intensity

For example, pepperoni pizza, steak tacos, or barbecued pork ribs.

fine-tuning
We're getting into medium to high tannins with Zinfandel. So it's a good idea to have some form of richness/meatiness/heaviness or slight bitterness in a recipe you pair with it—meats and other fatty

proteins, yes, but don't forget bitter elements like olives, citrus zest, bitter greens, and charring from grilling.

To balance both the tannins and the acidity, salt and acid in the food remain important.

And while spicy Zinfandel can handle somewhat spicy food, beware of more than medium heat. Combined with the sometimes-high alcohol level of Zinfandel, it could create too much of a burn.

other nuances

Once you have a pairing that's working on the basis of sweetness, acidity, tannins, weight, and intensity, you can start playing with subtler nuances.

Some of the subtle flavors that you might find in a Zinfandel include cherries, red berries (especially raspberries and cranberries), blackberries, plums, jam, pepper, baking spices (especially cloves), oak, and herbs. So it works to add those flavors, or foods that complement them, to your dishes.

other thoughts

Some foods that are considered classic pairings with Zinfandel are barbecue and barbecue sauce, steaks and chops, sausages, pizza, strong and aged cheeses, burgers, and grilled, stewed, or braised meats.

eggplant parmesan

Occasionally people will tell me that they don't like eggplant. I think it's mostly because it's easy to undercook eggplant, giving it the taste and texture of an old sponge.

Well prepared, however—which is best done with liberal use of olive oil—eggplant has a deliciously gloppy texture and a rich, earthy flavor. Add a crisped egg coating, hearty tomato sauce, and plenty of cheese and—what's not to love? • **Serves 6**

½ to ¾ cup extra virgin olive oil, divided
½ onion, cut into ¼-inch dice
4 cloves garlic, pressed through a garlic press or minced
One 28-ounce can crushed tomatoes
One 8-ounce can tomato sauce
¼ cup Zinfandel, or other dry red wine
½ teaspoon hot sauce, such as Tabasco
2 tablespoons chopped fresh oregano, divided
1 tablespoon coarse kosher salt, divided, plus more for sprinkling
¾ cup all-purpose flour
6 large eggs
4 teaspoons granulated garlic powder
10 tablespoons grated Parmesan cheese (3 to 4 ounces), divided
Eighteen ½-inch crosswise slices globe eggplant (about two 1-pound eggplants)
2 cups shredded mozzarella cheese (about 8 ounces), divided

■ In a large saucepan over medium heat, warm 2 tablespoons of the olive oil. Add the onion and cook, stirring occasionally, until tender, 4 to 6 minutes (adjust the heat, if necessary, to avoid browning). Add the minced garlic and cook, stirring occasionally, for 30 seconds. Stir in the tomatoes and tomato sauce, increase the heat to high, and bring to a boil. Remove from the heat and stir in the wine, hot sauce, 1 tablespoon of the oregano, and 1 teaspoon of the salt. (You can prepare the sauce in advance, storing it covered in the refrigerator for up to a week or in the freezer for several months. Thaw in the refrigerator before using.)

■ Place the flour in a shallow bowl. In a second shallow bowl, combine the eggs, garlic powder, ¼ cup of the Parmesan, and the remaining 2 teaspoons of salt, whisking to lightly beat the eggs and dissolve the salt.

■ In a large nonstick skillet over medium heat, warm ¼ cup of the remaining olive oil. One slice at a time, dip the eggplant slices in the flour, then the egg mixture, and add them to the skillet. Cook 4 to 6 slices at a time until lightly browned and tender, 2 to 4 minutes per side. Transfer the cooked slices to a paper towel–lined platter or plates and sprinkle with salt. Repeat with the remaining eggplant, wiping out the skillet and adding more oil as necessary.

■ Spray a 9 x 13-inch baking pan or casserole dish with nonstick cooking spray. Arrange one-third of the eggplant in the pan. Spoon about one-third of the tomato sauce on top of the slices and sprinkle with ⅔ cup of the mozzarella and 2 tablespoons of the remaining Parmesan. Make another layer using one-third of the eggplant, one-third of the tomato sauce, ⅔ cup of the mozzarella, and 2 tablespoons of the Parmesan. Finish with the remaining one-third of the eggplant and remaining one-third of the tomato sauce, making 6 layered stacks. (You can prepare the eggplant Parmesan up to a day in advance, storing it covered in the refrigerator. Return it to room temperature before proceeding.)

■ Preheat the oven to 350°F.

■ Bake until the eggplant stacks are heated through, about 40 minutes. Sprinkle the stacks with the remaining ⅔ cup of mozzarella and remaining 2 tablespoons of Parmesan and bake until the cheese is browned, about 10 minutes.

■ Transfer the stacks to a platter or plates. Sprinkle with the remaining 1 tablespoon of oregano, drizzle with any pan juices, and serve hot.

FOOD + WINE TIP You may have noticed that many of the recipes in this chapter have some form of tomatoes. That's no coincidence—Zin and tomatoes have a natural affinity.

an immigrant success story

Zinfandel was long thought to be America's, and even California's, own wine grape. But for years, researchers and growers had noticed a similarity to Italy's Primitivo. In the late 1990s, serious study began and, a few years and several DNA tests later, it was proved that Zinfandel and Primitivo are indeed the same grape—but one that actually hails from Croatia!

chicken rolls with prosciutto, fontina, and sun-dried tomatoes

Here's a recipe that's rustic, hearty, and yet refined—much like Zinfandel can be.

It's quick and easy enough for a weeknight, but also a great meal for company because you can prepare the chicken rolls in advance. About a half hour before serving, you give them a quick pan-sear, then finish them in the oven, leaving more time to spend with your guests. • **Serves 6**

- 6 large boneless, skinless chicken breasts (2½ to 3 pounds)
- 12 thin slices prosciutto (about 6 ounces)
- 1 tablespoon chopped fresh rosemary
- 1½ teaspoons coarse kosher salt
- ½ teaspoon freshly ground black pepper
- 4 ounces fontina cheese, shredded (you should have about 1½ cups)
- ¾ cup drained oil-packed sun-dried tomatoes, roughly chopped
- 2 tablespoons extra virgin olive oil

▓ Remove the tenders from the chicken breasts (save them for another use). Arrange the breasts, smooth side up, on a work surface and use a meat pounder to pound them to a uniform thickness, between ¼ and ½ inch.

▓ Lay a slice of prosciutto on top of each piece of chicken (it's okay if the prosciutto is bigger than the chicken). Turn the chicken over (so that the prosciutto is on the bottom) and lay another slice of prosciutto on top of each piece of chicken. Sprinkle with the rosemary, salt, and pepper. Arrange the cheese and sun-dried tomatoes on top. Starting at the wider end, roll each breast up, securing it with a toothpick. (You can prepare the chicken rolls up to 4 hours in advance, storing them covered in the refrigerator. Return them to room temperature before proceeding.)

▓ Preheat the oven to 400°F.

▓ In a very large ovenproof skillet over medium-high heat, warm the olive oil. (If you don't have an ovenproof skillet large enough to hold the chicken without crowding, use one large and one small or two medium ovenproof skillets, dividing the olive oil between them.) Add the chicken, seam side up, and cook until browned, about 4 minutes. Turn the chicken and place the skillet in the oven. Bake until the chicken is cooked through, 15 to 18 minutes. Let the breasts rest, loosely covered with foil, for 5 minutes.

▓ Serve the chicken with any pan juices drizzled on top. (Warn your guests about the toothpicks.)

chorizo sloppy joes

My husband grew up enjoying his mother's homemade Sloppy Joes, and they're still a favorite at her dinner table. I took that basic recipe and gave it a Latin twist. The result is a zippy new way to enjoy a retro favorite. Thanks, Mom. • **Serves 4**

  8 ounces 85 to 93 percent lean ground beef
  6 to 8 ounces Mexican pork or beef chorizo (see below), casings removed
  1 large onion, cut into ½-inch dice
  1 russet potato (about 12 ounces), cut into ¼-inch dice
    (you should have about 2⅓ cups)
    One 14.5-ounce can diced fire-roasted tomatoes
  1 cup reduced-sodium chicken broth
    One 8.75-ounce can red kidney beans, drained and rinsed
  1 tablespoon tomato paste
1½ teaspoons coarse kosher salt
  1 teaspoon granulated garlic powder
  4 hamburger buns, split horizontally
  ¾ cup corn kernels, fresh or frozen, thawed if frozen
  4 teaspoons cornstarch dissolved in 2 tablespoons cold water
  ¾ cup sour cream

■ In a large skillet over medium-high heat, cook the beef and chorizo, breaking them up with a spatula or spoon, for 1 minute. Add the onion and cook, stirring occasionally, for 3 minutes. Add the potato and cook, stirring occasionally, until the beef is browned, about 4 minutes. Stir in the tomatoes (with their juices), broth, kidney beans, tomato paste, salt, and garlic powder, scraping up any browned bits on the bottom of the skillet. Bring to a boil, reduce to a simmer, cover, and cook until the onion and potato are tender, about 20 minutes.

■ Meanwhile, preheat the broiler. Arrange a rack 4 to 6 inches from the heat. Arrange the buns, cut side up, on a rimmed baking sheet. Toast until lightly browned, 2 to 3 minutes.

■ Add the corn kernels and the cornstarch mixture to the skillet and cook, stirring, until the sauce thickens, 30 to 60 seconds.

■ Place 2 bun halves on each plate, cut side up. Top with the Sloppy Joe mixture and sour cream, dividing both evenly, and serve hot.

> **NOTE** Mexican chorizo is a raw sausage product, as opposed to Spanish chorizo, which is cooked and firm. Avoid ones meant to be enjoyed as Bratwurst-type sausages. Besides using it in this recipe, you can use chorizo in scrambled eggs, burritos, chili, and other Latin-inspired dishes.

FOOD + WINE TIP If the dish, combined with sometimes-high-alcohol Zinfandel, is too spicy for you, add a little more sour cream. That should temper things.

zinfandel chicken marbella

Here's a red wine riff on the Silver Palate's crowd-pleasing, amazingly easy to prepare Chicken Marbella. The resulting dish is satisfyingly fruity and bright, yet fantastically Zinfandel friendly. • **Serves 6 to 8**

½ cup Zinfandel, or other dry red wine
¼ cup extra virgin olive oil
¼ cup red wine vinegar
½ small orange, halved lengthwise (into quarters) and cut into ¼-inch slices (peel and all)
½ small lemon, halved lengthwise (into quarters) and cut into ¼-inch slices (peel and all)
½ cup raisins
½ cup pitted kalamata olives, halved
¼ cup drained capers, plus 1 tablespoon packing liquid
4 bay leaves
6 cloves garlic, thinly sliced
2 tablespoons chopped fresh rosemary
2 teaspoons coarse kosher salt
1 teaspoon freshly ground black pepper
Two 3½- to 4-pound chickens, cut into pieces
¼ cup packed light brown sugar

▓ In a large bowl, combine the wine, olive oil, vinegar, orange, lemon, raisins, olives, capers, caper packing liquid, bay leaves, garlic, rosemary, salt, and pepper.

▓ Divide the chicken between two large resealable bags, divide the olive oil mixture between them, and seal, squeezing out as much air as possible. Set aside in the refrigerator for 12 to 24 hours, turning occasionally.

▓ Preheat the oven to 350°F. Arrange one rack in the bottom third of the oven and another in the middle.

▓ Arrange the chicken, skin side up, in a single layer on two rimmed baking sheets. Squeeze the marinade mixture, including the fruit, olives, and capers, out of the bag and over the chicken, dividing it evenly. Sprinkle the brown sugar on top and bake, basting every 15 or 20 minutes, until the chicken is cooked through, 50 to 60 minutes. (You can prepare the chicken a day in advance, storing it covered in the refrigerator. Reheat in the juices or serve at room temperature.)

▓ Use a slotted spoon to transfer the chicken, fruit, olives, and capers to a platter or plates. Spoon some of the pan juices on top. Serve hot or at room temperature, passing any remaining pan juices at the table.

garlicky pepperoni pizza with fresh basil

My husband's and my favorite place to go for pizza is Tommaso's in San Francisco's North Beach, where the pepperoni pizza is absolutely to-die-for. Since moving to Napa, we get to Tommaso's less often—so we've had to learn how to make great pizza at home. It's not quite the same as North Beach, but it's definitely the next best thing.

I recommend Hormel pepperoni, which isn't as spicy as other brands. Zinfandel can sometimes be very high in alcohol, giving you a slight burn at the back of the throat—if your pepperoni is very spicy, it can exacerbate that burn, creating too much of a good thing.

A couple of tips for shaping pizza dough. First of all, gently coax it—working fast and furiously can make dough resist you. And second, if it does resist, just set it aside for a bit. Letting dough relax, repeatedly if necessary, will help. • **Serves 3 or 4**

1 ounce Parmesan cheese
One 12-ounce pizza dough, homemade (recipe follows) or store-bought
½ cup pizza sauce, homemade (recipe follows) or store-bought
4 cloves garlic, pressed through a garlic press or minced
1 cup shredded mozzarella cheese (about 4 ounces)
About 24 thin slices pepperoni (1½ to 2½ ounces)
3 tablespoons chopped fresh basil

▓ Use a vegetable peeler to cut the Parmesan into thick shaves (you should have about ⅓ cup). (You can shave the Parmesan up to a day in advance, storing it covered in the refrigerator.)

▓ Preheat the oven, along with a pizza stone if you have one, to 500°F.

▓ On a lightly floured surface, roll or stretch the dough out to a 12- to 14-inch round. Transfer the dough to a pizza pan or a flour- or cornmeal-dusted pizza paddle. Top with the pizza sauce, garlic, mozzarella, pepperoni, and Parmesan. Transfer the pizza to the oven and bake until the pizza is golden and crisp, 10 to 12 minutes.

▓ Sprinkle the pizza with the basil, cut into wedges, and serve.

FOOD + WINE TIP Although it's not a wine covered in this book, Chianti would also go well with pepperoni pizza.

homemade pizza dough

• **Makes one 12-ounce pizza dough**

This recipe yields a wonderfully sweet and chewy dough. The secret is a slow rise, overnight in the refrigerator.

You can double or triple the recipe for more pizzas. Divide the dough after you've let it sit overnight, then store the individual dough balls in resealable bags.

¼ teaspoon active dry yeast
1⅔ cups all-purpose flour
1 teaspoon coarse kosher salt

Place 2 tablespoons of warm water (118°F to 120°F) in the bowl of an electric mixer that has a dough hook attachment. Sprinkle the yeast on top of the water and set aside for 15 minutes (the mixture might not get foamy).

Add the flour, salt, and ½ cup of cool water. Use the dough hook to mix on medium-low speed for 4 minutes. Let the dough rest for 5 minutes, then mix again on medium-low for 3 minutes. The dough should be smooth and slightly sticky.

Place the dough in a lightly oiled bowl, rolling it to coat. Cover the bowl with plastic wrap, let it sit at room temperature for 30 minutes, then refrigerate it overnight. (You can prepare the dough in advance, storing it covered in the refrigerator for up to 2 days or in the freezer for several months.)

Return the dough to room temperature before using.

homemade pizza sauce

• **Makes about 1¾ cups, enough for four 12- to 14-inch pizzas**

If you like, freeze the sauce in four scant half-cup portions—each will be perfect for saucing one pizza.

One 14.5-ounce can diced tomatoes
¼ cup tomato paste
2 cloves garlic
2 teaspoons red wine vinegar
1 teaspoon coarsely chopped fresh oregano
1 teaspoon coarse kosher salt
⅛ teaspoon freshly ground black pepper
⅛ teaspoon cayenne pepper

In the bowl of a food processor, combine the tomatoes (with their juices), tomato paste, garlic, vinegar, oregano, salt, pepper, and cayenne and pulse to puree, scraping down the bowl as necessary. (You can prepare the pizza sauce in advance, storing it covered in the refrigerator for a week or in the freezer for up to several months. Thaw in the refrigerator before using.)

spice-rubbed pork chops with grilled tomato sauce

You won't believe how mouthwateringly flavorful these chops are, thanks to a deceptively simple rub and an amazing sauce.

If you have the time, brine the chops, and then to let the rub sit on the meat for an hour or two. If not, just sprinkle on the rub and grill.

While you're at it, toss some quartered bell peppers or halved zucchini on the grate—they'd be good alongside. • **Serves 4**

1 tablespoon smoked paprika (see note on page 73)
1 tablespoon chili powder
1½ teaspoons granulated garlic powder
1½ teaspoons granulated onion powder
1 teaspoon chopped fresh thyme
2¾ to 4 teaspoons coarse kosher salt, divided, or more to taste
4 pork rib chops, about 1 inch thick, ideally brined (see page 81)
½ onion (halved through the root end)
4 plum tomatoes, halved lengthwise and seeded
1 tablespoon extra virgin olive oil
1 tablespoon tomato paste
1½ teaspoons red wine vinegar, or more to taste

■ In a shallow bowl, combine the paprika, chili powder, garlic powder, onion powder, thyme, and 1¼ teaspoons of the salt (or 2½ teaspoons if you didn't brine). Arrange the pork on a platter or large plate in a single layer and sprinkle the rub on both sides. Cover and refrigerate for 1 to 2 hours.

■ Return the pork to room temperature.

■ Keeping the root end intact, cut the onion into 6 wedges. In a large bowl, toss the onion, tomatoes, olive oil, and remaining 1½ teaspoons of salt. Set aside.

■ Prepare the grill to medium-high heat and lightly oil the grate. Grill the pork until cooked through, about 6 minutes per side. Grill the onion until softened and lightly charred, 4 to 5 minutes per side. Grill the tomatoes, skin side down, until softened and lightly charred, about 2 minutes. Transfer the pork to a platter or plates and let it rest, loosely covered with foil, for 5 minutes.

■ Meanwhile, in the bowl of a food processor, combine the onion, tomatoes, tomato paste, and vinegar and pulse to puree, scraping down the bowl as necessary. Taste, ideally with your wine, and add more salt and/or vinegar if you like.

■ Serve the pork chops in a pool of tomato sauce, drizzled with any accumulated juices.

tipsy tri-tip

There's nothing more all-American than throwing a succulent slab of beef on the grill and slathering it with barbecue sauce. Here, the meat gets extra oomph from a twelve- to twenty-four-hour marinade containing both Zinfandel and whiskey, which also flavor the sauce.

You might think all that alcohol would make the dish too boozy. But once it gets reduced down, the wine adds a nice brightness and the whiskey, an ever-so-slight caramel flavor. • **Serves 8**

- ¾ cup extra virgin olive oil
- 1 small red onion, cut into chunks
- 6 cloves garlic
- 2 tablespoons coarse kosher salt
- 1½ cups Zinfandel, or other dry red wine
- ¾ cup whiskey
- ¼ cup red wine vinegar
  Two 2-pound beef tri-tip roasts, excess fat trimmed
- 6 tablespoons ketchup
- 3 tablespoons tomato paste
- 2 tablespoons honey

▦ In the bowl of a food processor, combine the olive oil, onion, garlic, and salt and process to puree, scraping down the bowl as necessary. Add the wine, whiskey, and vinegar and process to blend, scraping down the bowl as necessary. (You can prepare the marinade up to 3 days in advance, storing it covered in the refrigerator.)

▦ Place each tri-tip roast in a large resealable bag, add the marinade, dividing it evenly, and seal, squeezing out as much air as possible. Set aside in the refrigerator for 12 to 24 hours, turning occasionally.

▦ Remove the tri-tips from the marinade (save the marinade), pat them dry, and set aside. Transfer the marinade to a large saucepan. Stir in the ketchup, tomato paste, and honey and bring to a boil over high heat. Cook, stirring occasionally, until reduced to 2½ cups, 35 to 50 minutes, depending on the saucepan (adjust the heat, if necessary, to avoid boiling over and/or splattering). Set aside.

▦ Prepare the grill to medium-high heat and lightly oil the grate. Grill the tri-tips to a few minutes shy of desired doneness, about 8 minutes per side for medium rare. Liberally brush the tri-tips with the wine sauce and cook for another minute per side. Repeat two more times, for a total of about 11 minutes per side for medium rare. Transfer the tri-tips to a cutting board and let them rest, loosely covered with foil, for 10 minutes.

▦ Cut the meat across the grain into thin slices and serve hot. Pass the remaining wine sauce at the table.

syrah

S yrah is smoky and inky and fruity. It can have hints of leather and spice and cocoa. And it's often described as meaty.

Syrah also comes from the same part of France, the Rhône Valley, that's home to Viognier, a wine full of exotic elegance. Yet Syrah is quite the opposite, earthy and kind of low down and dirty—and I mean that in a good way.

But perhaps best of all, almost every Syrah pairing is improved by the addition of bacon. How could you not love a wine for which that is so?

syrah by another name

• **Shiraz.** This is the name for the same grape in Australia. • **Rhône wines.** As with other French wines, these French Syrahs are labeled with the name of the area they're from. They might have the general area name Rhône Valley, or names of subregions within the Rhône (Côte-Rôtie, for example). Basically, any red wine from the northern Rhône will be 100 percent Syrah, while any red wine from the southern Rhône will be a blend of mostly Syrah and Grenache.

pairing with syrah

Although there are, of course, nuances to Syrah, the most important factors in food and wine pairing aren't a wine's nuances, but its broad strokes. If you learn a wine's overall characteristics and combine that information with the General Pairing Tips (page 8), you'll have a near-perfect pairing every time.

Broad characteristics:
• dry (not sweet)
• medium to high in acidity, crispness, or brightness
• medium to high in tannins
• heavy weight
• strong intensity

Pairs well with dishes that are:
• not sweet
• medium to high in acidity, crispness, or brightness
• medium to high in richness/meatiness/heaviness, acidity, or slight bitterness
• heavy weight
• strong intensity

For example, marinated grilled steak, wine-braised short ribs, or garlic-rosemary leg of lamb.

fine-tuning

Syrah's uniquely meaty flavors, along with even more tannins in the wine, mean that your pairings will be helped by even more meatiness in the food. Go with meats that are similarly earthy—grilled meats, cured meats, spicy meats. You can also use other "meaty" ingredients—like sun-dried tomatoes, olives, and cheese.

Still, salt and acid remain key. As with Merlot, which has dark fruit flavors like Syrah, balsamic vinegar is a great tool.

other nuances

Once you have a pairing that's working on the basis of sweetness, acidity, tannins, weight, and intensity, you can start playing with subtler nuances.

In addition to the meatiness mentioned above, some of the subtle flavors that you might find in a Syrah include dark berries (especially blackberries, boysenberries, and black currants), black cherries, black olives, bacon, pepper, baking spices (especially cloves), smoke, cocoa, and herbs. So it works to add those flavors, or foods that complement them, to your dishes.

other thoughts

Some foods that are considered classic pairings with Syrah are beef, lamb, barbecue and barbecue sauce, grilled foods, braised dishes and stews, sausages, mushrooms, aged and hard cheeses, and tuna steak.

smoky lentil and vegetable stew

Here's a hearty, warming stew brimming with colorful vegetables and chewy bits of bacon. To make it vegetarian, simply omit the bacon and use vegetable broth. • **Serves 6 to 8**

6 thick slices bacon, cut crosswise into ½-inch strips (optional)
2 tablespoons extra virgin olive oil (if not using bacon)
1 red bell pepper, cored, seeded, and cut into ½-inch dice
1 yellow bell pepper, cored, seeded, and cut into ½-inch dice
1 onion, cut into ½-inch dice
4 cloves garlic, pressed through a garlic press or minced
4 teaspoons smoked paprika (see note on page 73)
2 teaspoons coarse kosher salt
6 cups reduced-sodium chicken or vegetable broth
1¼ cups lentils
2 tablespoons soy sauce
2 crookneck squash or yellow zucchini, quartered lengthwise and cut into ½-inch slices
2 zucchini, quartered lengthwise and cut into ½-inch slices
2 cups small broccoli florets
2 cups small cauliflower florets
2 teaspoons chopped fresh marjoram (see note on page 107), divided
2 teaspoons chopped fresh thyme, divided
   One 14.5-ounce can diced fire-roasted tomatoes, drained
½ cup Syrah, or other dry red wine

▨ In a large stockpot over medium-low heat, cook the bacon, if using, stirring occasionally, until crisp, about 10 minutes. Use a slotted spoon to transfer the bacon to a large bowl. Set aside to cool. (If not using bacon, in a large stockpot over medium-high heat, warm the olive oil.)

▨ If necessary, increase the heat under the stockpot to medium-high. Add the bell peppers and onion and cook, stirring occasionally, for 2 minutes. Add the garlic, paprika, and salt and cook, stirring occasionally, until the garlic is fragrant, about 1 minute.

▨ Stir in the broth, lentils, and soy sauce. Increase the heat to high, bring to a boil, and reduce to a simmer. Cook 10 minutes. Add the squash, zucchini, broccoli, cauliflower, 1 teaspoon of the marjoram, and 1 teaspoon of the thyme. Increase the heat to high, bring to a boil, and reduce to a simmer. Cook until the lentils and vegetables are tender, 10 to 15 minutes. Add the tomatoes, wine, and bacon and cook, stirring, until the tomatoes are heated through, 1 to 2 minutes.

▨ Serve hot, garnished with the remaining 1 teaspoon of marjoram and remaining 1 teaspoon of thyme.

tapenade swordfish skewers with warm edamame bulgur salad

It's super-easy to make tapenade. Just put your ingredients in the food processor and—buzz, buzz, buzz—it's done! Here, the mixture is slightly vinegary, which helps the finished dish stand up to the wine.

Look for bulgur wheat in the bulk foods section of your supermarket. Or buy a packaged tabbouleh mix and use the bulgur that's in the package, ignoring the seasoning mix.

And the best place to find sustainable swordfish is a good fishmonger. • **Serves 6**

¾ cup drained pitted kalamata olives
2 tablespoons balsamic vinegar, or more to taste
2 tablespoons red wine vinegar, or more to taste
4 teaspoons extra virgin olive oil
2½ teaspoons coarse kosher salt, or more to taste
2 teaspoons freshly ground black pepper, or more to taste
1½ to 1¾ pounds swordfish steaks, skin removed, cut into 1- to 1½-inch pieces
1 cup bulgur wheat
1 cup shelled edamame beans, thawed if frozen
½ cup coarsely chopped fresh mint
Special equipment: skewers, soaked in water for at least 10 minutes if they're wood or bamboo

■ In the bowl of a food processor, combine the olives, vinegars, olive oil, salt, and pepper and pulse to make a coarse puree, scraping down the bowl as necessary. (You can prepare the tapenade up to 3 days in advance, storing it covered in the refrigerator. Return it to room temperature before serving.)

■ Place the fish in a medium bowl and add about half of the tapenade, tossing to coat. Set aside to marinate at room temperature for 30 minutes. In a large bowl, combine the remaining tapenade, bulgur wheat, edamame, mint, and 1⅓ cups of boiling water. Cover and set aside for 30 minutes, or until ready to serve.

■ Prepare the grill to medium-high heat and lightly oil the grate. Arrange the fish on skewers. Grill until cooked through, about 3 minutes per side.

■ Taste the bulgur salad, ideally with your wine, and add more vinegar, salt, and/or pepper if you like. Arrange the bulgur salad on a platter or plates. Top with the swordfish skewers and serve hot.

FOOD + WINE TIP Contrary to the "red with meat, white with fish" rule, Syrah and a meaty fish, like swordfish or tuna, is a great pairing.

moroccan-spiced cornish hens and roasted root vegetables

Perfumed with bold and exotic spices yet dead simple to make, these little hens will wow you—along with everyone else at the table. Both ginger and pepper in the rub give the dish a warm, bordering-on-hot quality, but only enough to complement the sometimes-spicy, peppery nature of the wine. • **Serves 4**

4 teaspoons ground cinnamon
4 teaspoons ground coriander
4 teaspoons ground ginger
1 tablespoon coarse kosher salt
2 teaspoons freshly ground black pepper
1 teaspoon ground nutmeg, preferably freshly grated
¼ cup extra virgin olive oil, divided
12 small red potatoes (about 1 pound), cut into ½-inch wedges
8 ounces carrots, thicker parts halved lengthwise, cut into ¼-inch slices (you should have about 1¼ cups)
8 ounces parsnips, thicker parts halved lengthwise, cut into ¼-inch slices (you should have about 1¼ cups)
Two 1¼- to 1½-pound Cornish hens

▦ Preheat the oven to 450°F. Spray a 9 x 13-inch baking pan with nonstick cooking spray.

▦ In a small bowl, combine the cinnamon, coriander, ginger, salt, pepper, and nutmeg. Stir in 3 tablespoons of the olive oil to make a paste. In a medium bowl, combine 1 tablespoon of the paste with the remaining 1 tablespoon of olive oil. Add the potatoes, carrots, and parsnips, tossing to evenly coat. Transfer the mixture to the prepared baking pan.

▦ Spread the remaining paste all over the hens. Tie the legs together and tuck in the wings. Set the hens, breast side up, on the vegetables. Roast until the hens are cooked through and the vegetables are tender, 40 to 45 minutes. Transfer the hens to a cutting board and let them rest, loosely covered with foil, for 10 minutes.

▦ Meanwhile, toss the vegetables and return them to the oven. Roast until browned, about 10 minutes.

▦ Halve or quarter the hens and serve them hot, with the roasted vegetables on the side.

mega-meat calzone with three cheeses

As the recipe title promises, this calzone is jam-packed with meaty goodness. The accompanying cheese filling will be nicely oozy if you use whole milk mozzarella and ricotta—but part-skim will work as well. For tips on working with pizza dough, see page 153. • **Serves 4**

  2 mild Italian sausages (6 to 7 ounces), casings removed
1½ cups shredded mozzarella cheese (about 6 ounces)
  1 cup ricotta cheese (about 8 ounces)
¼ cup shredded Parmesan cheese (about ¾ ounce)
  4 teaspoons chopped fresh oregano
  3 cloves garlic, pressed through a garlic press or minced
¾ teaspoon coarse kosher salt
¼ teaspoon freshly ground black pepper
    One 12-ounce pizza dough, homemade (recipe on page 153) or store-bought
 12 thin slices coppa (sometimes called capicola) (1½ to 2½ ounces) (see below)
 12 thin slices Italian dry salami (1½ to 2½ ounces)

■ In a small skillet over medium heat, cook the sausage, breaking it up with a spatula or spoon, until cooked through, 5 to 7 minutes. Set aside to cool.

■ In a medium bowl, combine the mozzarella, ricotta, Parmesan, oregano, garlic, salt, and pepper. Set aside. (You can prepare the sausage and the cheese mixture up to a day in advance, storing them covered in the refrigerator.)

■ Preheat the oven to 400°F. Dust a rimmed baking sheet with flour or cornmeal.

■ Divide the dough in half and shape each half into a ball. On a lightly floured surface, roll or stretch each ball out to a 9-inch round. Transfer the rounds to the prepared baking sheet.

■ Crumble one-third of the cheese mixture over half of each of the rounds, dividing it evenly, leaving a ¾-inch border. Top with the coppa, another one-third of the cheese mixture, the salami, the remaining one-third of the cheese mixture, and the sausage. Fold the uncovered dough over the filling and pinch the edges together to firmly seal, forming two half circles. Make 3 small slits on the top of each calzone.

■ Bake until golden brown, about 30 minutes. Serve hot.

NOTE Coppa, sometimes called capicola, is similar to prosciutto in that it's air-dried, cured pork, but because it comes from a different part of the animal, it yields round slices. It's increasingly available at the deli counter of better markets and specialty food stores, but if you can't find it, substitute thinly sliced prosciutto, cut into ¼-inch strips.

garlic rosemary rack of lamb

Simple. Classic. Delicious. Rack of lamb is all that and more—including quite easy to prepare.

In this recipe, the garlic roasts to a mellow deliciousness, the rosemary complements the typically herbaceous notes in the wine, and a touch of balsamic ties it all together.

To help the pairing be all it can be, don't be too aggressive trimming the racks' fat—that richness is a pairing plus! • **Serves 4**

- 1 cup fresh rosemary leaves, plus sprigs for garnish
- 12 cloves garlic
- 4 teaspoons coarse kosher salt
- 2 teaspoons freshly ground black pepper
- 2 teaspoons balsamic vinegar
- ¼ cup extra virgin olive oil, divided
  Two 1¼- to 1½-pound racks of lamb, ideally frenched, excess fat trimmed

In the bowl of a food processor, combine the rosemary leaves, garlic, salt, and pepper and pulse to finely chop, scraping down the bowl as necessary. Add the vinegar and 2 tablespoons of the olive oil and pulse to make a coarse, wet paste, scraping down the bowl as necessary.

Arrange the lamb on a rimmed baking sheet and spread the paste all over the racks (including the boney side). Cover and refrigerate for 8 to 24 hours (see note on page 139).

Return the lamb to room temperature.

Preheat the oven to 450°F.

Meanwhile, in a large skillet over high heat, warm the remaining 2 tablespoons of olive oil. Add 1 rack, meaty side down, and cook until well seared, about 2 minutes. Return the rack to the baking sheet, meaty side up. Repeat with the remaining rack.

Roast until an internal thermometer reads 130°F for medium rare, 15 to 20 minutes. Transfer the lamb to a cutting board and let it rest, loosely covered with foil, for 15 minutes. (It will continue to cook, reaching an internal temperature of about 140°F.)

Cut each rack into 4 double chops. Serve hot, drizzled with any accumulated juices and garnished with the rosemary sprigs.

FOOD + WINE TIP Fatty meats—like lamb, steaks, sausages, and salami—have a natural affinity to big, typically tannic wines like Syrah and Cabernet Sauvignon. The tannins help cut through the richness of the meat, while the fat helps to mellow the bitterness of the tannins.

open-faced salami-focaccia melt

I recently went to a food and wine pairing party at my friend Andrea's, where a version of this sandwich was my favorite dish. It's familiarly pizza-like, but studded with deliciously creative toppings. • **Serves 6**

Half of a 9 x 12-inch loaf focaccia bread, homemade (recipe follows) or store-bought, or 3 ciabatta buns
¼ cup shredded Asiago cheese (about 1 ounce)
¼ cup mayonnaise
1½ teaspoons Dijon mustard
8 ounces fresh mozzarella cheese, shredded (you should have about 2 cups), divided
10 ounces thinly sliced Italian dry salami
½ cup roughly chopped pitted kalamata olives
¼ cup thinly sliced red onion
One 4-ounce can diced green chiles, drained
1 tablespoon chopped fresh flat-leaf parsley

■ If using focaccia, cut the bread into 3 pieces, then cut each piece in half horizontally. If using ciabatta buns, cut each bun in half horizontally. Spray a rimmed baking sheet with nonstick cooking spray and arrange the bread, cut side up, on the sheet.

■ Preheat the broiler. Arrange a rack about 6 inches from the heat.

■ In a small bowl, combine the Asiago, mayonnaise, and mustard. Spread the mixture on the cut sides of the bread. Top with two-thirds of the mozzarella, dividing it evenly. Top with the salami, olives, onion, chiles, and remaining one-third of the mozzarella, dividing them evenly. Broil until the cheese melts, 3 to 5 minutes.

■ Sprinkle with the parsley and serve hot.

how to learn a lot without spending a lot

Pick a wine variety you want to know better, invite a few friends over, and ask each of them to bring a bottle of the wine. Prepare a recipe or two from this book that go with the wine you'll be tasting.

Once everyone arrives, open all the bottles and try the wines. Notice each wine's overall characteristics—its sweetness (or lack thereof), acidity, tannins, weight, and intensity. Also make note of the wine's nuances—its flavors and aromas.

Once you've tasted four to six bottles, you'll start to get a sense of the wine variety and what you can generally expect when you buy a bottle of it, any bottle of it.

After the initial tasting, bring in the food, enjoy it with the wine, and discuss what you've noticed. Repeat the party, perhaps rotating hosts, for as many types of wines as you're interested in.

homemade focaccia bread

• **Makes one 9-by-12-inch loaf (about 1½ pounds)**

I used to own a small café in Sausalito, just across the Golden Gate Bridge from San Francisco, where our turkey sandwich was hands down the most popular item on the menu—a fact that I attribute to the excellent focaccia it was served on. Here's the recipe, which produces a loaf you can cut into four-inch squares and split open horizontally for sandwich bread, or cut into sticks for dipping.

The recipe doesn't need a lot of hands-on time, but it does need to be started at least a day before you plan to bake it.

   2 teaspoons active dry yeast, divided
2¾ plus ⅔ cups all-purpose flour, divided
   ¼ cup extra virgin olive oil, divided, plus more for the bowl and baking sheet
   2 tablespoons plus ½ teaspoon coarse kosher salt, divided

Place ½ cup of warm water (118°F to 120°F) in a medium bowl. Sprinkle 1 teaspoon of the yeast on top of the water and set aside for 15 minutes (the mixture might not get foamy).

Stir in ⅔ cup of the flour. Loosely cover the bowl with plastic wrap and set aside at room temperature for 45 minutes.

Place 2 tablespoons of warm water (118°F to 120°F) in the bowl of an electric mixer that has a dough hook attachment. Sprinkle the remaining 1 teaspoon of yeast on top of the water and set aside for 15 minutes (the mixture might not get foamy).

Add the flour mixture, 3 tablespoons of the olive oil, 2 tablespoons of the salt, and ⅔ cup of cool water to the mixer bowl and stir lightly. Add the remaining 2¾ cups of flour and use the dough hook to mix on medium-low speed for 2 minutes. Let the dough rest for 5 minutes, then mix again on medium-low for 4 minutes. The dough should be smooth and slightly sticky.

Place the dough in a lightly oiled bowl, rolling it to coat. Cover the bowl with plastic wrap, let it sit at room temperature for 30 minutes, then refrigerate it overnight. (You can prepare the dough in advance, storing it covered in the refrigerator for up to 2 days or in the freezer for several months. Thaw in the refrigerator before proceeding.)

Coat a rimmed baking sheet with olive oil. Place the dough on the baking sheet and gently coax it into about an 8 x 10-inch rectangle. Lightly cover the dough with plastic wrap and set it aside at room temperature until it expands to about 9 x 12 inches and is about 1½ inches tall, about 2 hours.

Preheat the oven to 400°F.

Uncover the dough and use your fingertips to deeply dimple it. Drizzle the dough with the remaining 1 tablespoon of olive oil, then sprinkle it with the remaining ½ teaspoon of salt. Bake the focaccia until nicely browned, 25 to 30 minutes. Transfer the baking pan with the focaccia to a wire rack to cool for 10 minutes. Remove the focaccia from the baking pan and return it to the wire rack to cool completely. (You can prepare the focaccia in advance, storing it covered in the freezer for up to a month. Thaw at room temperature before serving.)

big beef ribs with syrah sauce

If you've never had beef ribs, you're in for a treat. They're big, like something Fred Flintstone would eat. Compared to pork ribs, the meat is less mild, with bold flavor and beefy richness. And in this recipe—cooked slowly on the grill, but not so slowly that they take hours to prepare—they're both juicy and crisp, begging to be eaten with your fingers. Have plenty of napkins on hand, and plenty of Syrah.

Some supermarkets sell beef back ribs separately—they're the same bones as in a standing rib roast—but many don't. Try calling ahead and, if necessary, order them from a butcher. • **Serves 4 to 6**

- 2 tablespoons dried oregano
- 4 teaspoons ground coriander
- 4 teaspoons ground cumin
- 2 teaspoons coarse kosher salt
- 1 teaspoon granulated garlic powder
- 1 teaspoon granulated onion powder
- ¾ teaspoon ground cinnamon
- ½ teaspoon cayenne pepper
- 7 to 8 pounds beef back ribs (about 12 ribs), excess fat trimmed
- ¾ cup Syrah, or other dry red wine
- ¼ cup balsamic vinegar
- ½ cup packed light brown sugar
- 2 tablespoons Dijon mustard

■ In a small bowl, combine the oregano, coriander, cumin, salt, garlic powder, onion powder, cinnamon, and cayenne. Arrange the ribs on a rimmed baking sheet (it's okay if they overlap) and rub all over with the spice mixture. Cover and refrigerate for 8 to 24 hours (see note on page 139).

■ Meanwhile, in a medium saucepan over medium-high heat, combine the wine, vinegar, brown sugar, and mustard, whisking to dissolve the sugar. Bring to a boil and cook until the mixture is reduced to ½ cup, about 5 minutes (adjust the heat, if necessary, to avoid boiling over). Remove from the heat and set aside.

■ Return the ribs to room temperature.

■ Prepare the grill to medium-low heat and lightly oil the grate. Grill the ribs, covered, turning occasionally and moving the ribs, if necessary, to avoid flare-ups, until lightly charred and the thickest part of a rib is fork-tender, about 35 minutes. Transfer to a cutting board and let the ribs rest, loosely covered with foil, for 10 minutes.

■ Cut the ribs into one-rib pieces and transfer to a platter or plates. Serve hot, with the wine sauce on the side or drizzled on top.

bacon-wrapped filet mignon with blackberries

These steaks have got it going on. Smoky, savory bacon. Bright, tart berries. And a flavorful pan sauce that sends it home. Your table-mates will be begging for the recipe. • **Serves 8**

    8 thick slices bacon
      Eight 6- to 7-ounce filet mignon medallions, about 1½ inches thick
 2½ teaspoons coarse kosher salt, divided, or more to taste
 1¼ teaspoons freshly ground black pepper, divided, or more to taste
    1 tablespoon extra virgin olive oil
    4 shallots, cut into ¼-inch dice (you should have about ¾ cup)
 1½ teaspoons chopped fresh rosemary
    ½ cup Syrah, or other dry red wine
    2 cups blackberries, divided
    2 tablespoons (¼ stick) unsalted butter, cut into 2 or 3 pieces

■ In two medium skillets over medium-low heat, cook the bacon, turning occasionally, until just beginning to turn golden, about 6 minutes. Transfer the bacon to a paper towel–lined plate and set aside. Remove the skillets from the heat (but don't drain the bacon fat).

■ Once the bacon is cool enough to handle, wrap the outside edge of each filet with a slice, forming a ring around the filet, and secure the bacon with a toothpick (it's okay if it doesn't reach all the way around). Sprinkle the filets on both sides with 2 teaspoons of the salt and 1 teaspoon of the pepper.

■ Rewarm the skillets over medium-high heat. Add the filets and cook to desired doneness, about 4½ minutes per side for medium rare. Transfer the filets to a platter or plates and let them rest, loosely covered with foil, for 5 minutes.

■ Meanwhile, add the olive oil to one of the skillets and warm it over medium-high heat (remove the other skillet from the heat). Add the shallots, rosemary, remaining ½ teaspoon of salt, and remaining ¼ teaspoon of pepper and cook, stirring occasionally, until the shallots are tender, about 1 minute. Stir in the wine and 1 cup of the blackberries, scraping up any browned bits on the bottom of the skillet, and cook until the liquid is reduced to a thin layer, about 1½ minutes. Remove from the heat, add the butter, and stir until it melts and most of the berries have broken up. Taste the sauce, ideally with your wine, and add more salt and/or pepper if you like.

■ Pour the sauce over the steaks. Garnish with the remaining 1 cup of blackberries and serve hot. (Warn your guests about the toothpicks.)

rib-eye steaks with green olive butter

Here's one of the world's easiest ways to dress up a steak, chop, chicken breast, or fish fillet—top it with a pat or two of flavored butter, which melts into the just-cooked food, enhancing it and making a simple sauce.

In this recipe, green olives in the butter make a briny, bright complement to a rich rib-eye, and the juxtaposition is an ideal match for the sometimes-vernal flavors in Syrah. • **Serves 6**

¼ cup drained pimento-stuffed Spanish olives (martini olives), plus more for garnish
12 fresh chives, cut into rough 1-inch pieces, plus whole chives for garnish
2 cloves garlic
2½ teaspoons coarse kosher salt, divided
1¼ teaspoons freshly ground black pepper, divided
4 tablespoons (½ stick) unsalted butter
Six 9- to 10-ounce rib-eye steaks, about 1 inch thick, excess fat trimmed
¼ cup extra virgin olive oil

▓ In the bowl of a food processor, combine the ¼ cup of olives, cut chives, garlic, ½ teaspoon of the salt, and ¼ teaspoon of the pepper and pulse to coarsely chop, scraping down the bowl as necessary. Add the butter and pulse to combine, scraping down the bowl as necessary. Transfer the green olive butter to a small bowl and set aside. (You can prepare the green olive butter in advance, storing it covered in the refrigerator for up to 3 days or in the freezer for several months. Return it to room temperature before proceeding.)

▓ Sprinkle both sides of the steaks with the remaining 2 teaspoons of salt and remaining 1 teaspoon of pepper.

▓ In each of two large skillets over medium-heat, warm 2 tablespoons of olive oil. Add the steaks and cook to desired doneness, about 3½ minutes per side for medium rare. Transfer the steaks to a platter or plates and top with the green olive butter, dividing it evenly. Let the steaks rest, loosely covered with foil, for 5 minutes.

▓ Serve the steaks hot, garnished with the olives and whole chives.

FOOD + WINE TIP If you like, grill your steak instead of pan-searing it. Either way, it'll work with the wine.

shallot and green peppercorn brisket

Brisket is a great do-ahead dish, because it actually tastes better a day or two later. This particular version gets Syrah-friendly flavor from green peppercorns, which add spicy notes without being overpowering, plus plenty of wine in the braising liquid. Oh, and roasted garlic cloves—are they ever not fantastic? • **Serves 6 to 8**

      One 4½- to 5-pound flat-cut beef brisket, excess fat trimmed
   8 shallots, cut into ½-inch dice
  12 cloves garlic, halved crosswise
   3 tablespoons green peppercorns (dried, not packed in brine) (see below)
   3 tablespoons chopped fresh thyme
   1 tablespoon granulated garlic powder
   4 teaspoons coarse kosher salt
   2 tablespoons extra virgin olive oil
      One 750-ml bottle Syrah, or other dry red wine
   3 tablespoons all-purpose flour

▧ Preheat the oven to 375°F.

▧ Arrange the brisket, fat side up, in a 9 x 13-inch baking pan (it's okay if it's a little cramped—the brisket will shrink as it cooks). Arrange the shallots and garlic around the brisket and bake, uncovered, for 30 minutes.

▧ Meanwhile, use a mortar and pestle to lightly crush the peppercorns. (If you don't have a mortar and pestle, place them in a small bowl and lightly crush them with the end of a wooden spoon.) Stir in the thyme, garlic powder, and salt. Stir in the olive oil, making a paste. In a separate bowl, combine the wine and flour, whisking to dissolve the flour.

▧ Remove the brisket from the oven (leave the oven on) and spread the peppercorn mixture on top. Pour the wine mixture in the pan around the meat. Cover tightly with foil and continue baking until the meat is very tender, about 3 hours. Remove the brisket from the oven and let it cool in the pan juices, uncovered, for 30 minutes.

▧ Transfer the brisket to a cutting board. Slice the meat across the grain and serve hot, with the sauce on the side. (You can prepare the brisket up to 2 days in advance. Cool it thoroughly in the pan juices, then store it covered in the refrigerator. Before reheating, slice the cold meat. Return the meat to the sauce, cover, and reheat in a preheated 350°F oven, about 45 minutes.)

NOTE **Dried green peppercorns** are available in the spice section at better supermarkets. Besides using them in this recipe, you can crush them and press them into steaks and chops, stir them into mayonnaise and aïoli, and sprinkle them over salads.

cabernet
sauvignon

We can wax poetic about other wine varieties, but let's face it. When you want to pull out all the stops, to serve a wine that's really special and that will lend a note of pomp and circumstance to the occasion, you almost always reach for Cabernet Sauvignon.

Perhaps it's because we have Cabernet to thank for the great wines of Bordeaux's Left Bank, possibly the best there are. We have Cabernet to thank for the acclaimed wines of California. Many of us have Cabernet to thank for first seducing us into the world of wine.

But I think it's also because, like a romance you just can't forget, Cabernet remains elusive, enigmatic, aloof. Mostly because of typically big, bold tannins, Cab keeps us at a distance.

In terms of food and wine pairing, that boldness means you have to narrow your aim a bit. But when you hit the target, a Cabernet pairing is that much more exciting, inspiring, and satisfying.

cabernet sauvignon by another name

• **Bordeaux, Red Bordeaux.** As with other French wines, these French Cabernet Sauvignon blends are labeled with the name of the area they're from. They might have the general name Bordeaux, or the names of subregions within Bordeaux (Médoc, for example). In blends from the Left Bank of Bordeaux, Cabernet will be the dominant grape. On the Right Bank, Cabernet Sauvignon will likely be part of the blend, but a minor player. • **Meritage.** A group of American vintners have trademarked this name, pronounced to rhyme with "heritage," for Bordeaux-style blends made in the United States. These wines often include Cabernet Sauvignon but may or may not be mostly Cab.

pairing with cabernet sauvignon

Although there are, of course, nuances to Cabernet Sauvignon, the most important factors in food and wine pairing aren't a wine's nuances, but its broad strokes. If you learn a wine's overall characteristics and combine that information with the General Pairing Tips (page 8), you'll have a near-perfect pairing every time.

Broad characteristics:
- dry (not sweet)
- medium to high in acidity, crispness, or brightness
- high in tannins
- heavy weight
- strong intensity

Pairs well with dishes that are:

- not sweet
- medium to high in acidity, crispness, or brightness
- high in richness/meatiness/heaviness, acidity, or slight bitterness
- heavy weight
- strong intensity

For example, prime rib, steak with blue cheese, or grilled lamb chops.

The biggest consideration, though, is the tannins. Make sure your dishes have enough meatiness, acidity, bitterness, and/or salt to work with Cabernet Sauvignon.

fine-tuning

Although there aren't a wide variety of foods that go with Cabernet Sauvignon, as long as you're using one or more of them, your pairings should sing.

Playing with salt and acid levels will help marry a dish to your particular bottle of Cab—Dijon mustard is a good acid choice, the severity of the mustard mimicking the severity of the wine. And don't forget rich/meaty/heavy elements—fatty meats like well-marbled steak, for example—and/or bitter elements, like charring, bitter greens, and walnuts or pecans.

other nuances

Once you have a pairing that's working on the basis of sweetness, acidity, tannins, weight, and intensity, you can start playing with subtler nuances.

Some of the subtle flavors that you might find in a Cabernet Sauvignon include dark berries (especially blackberries, boysenberries, and black currants), black cherries, green pepper, baking spices (especially cloves), cedar, tobacco, and eucalyptus. So it works to add those flavors, or foods that complement them, to your dishes.

other thoughts

Some foods that are considered classic pairings with Cabernet Sauvignon are beef in almost any form (especially steak and prime rib), lamb, venison, grilled foods, and aged, blue, and sometimes-stinky cheeses.

steak and radicchio caesar

You can definitely enjoy red wine with salad, especially if it's a bold, hearty salad like this one. • **Serves 4**

    1 ounce Parmesan cheese, plus 3 tablespoons grated Parmesan (about 1 ounce)
    3 tablespoons red wine vinegar
    2 cloves garlic
    1 tablespoon Dijon mustard
    2 teaspoons Worcestershire sauce
 1½ teaspoons anchovy paste
 1¼ teaspoons coarse kosher salt, divided, or more to taste
  ¾ teaspoon freshly ground black pepper, divided, or more to taste
  ⅓ cup extra virgin olive oil
   12 to 14 ounces boneless sirloin steak or flank steak, about ¾ inch thick
    1 small head romaine lettuce, cut or torn into bite-sized pieces
      (you should have about 6 cups)
    1 head radicchio, halved, cored, and cut into ¼-inch shreds
      (you should have about 5 cups)
    4 cups loosely packed arugula (about 2 ounces)
  ½ small red onion, halved lengthwise (into quarters) and thinly sliced
  ¼ cup drained oil-packed julienned sun-dried tomatoes

■ In a blender, combine the grated cheese, vinegar, garlic, mustard, Worcestershire, anchovy paste, ½ teaspoon of the salt, and ½ teaspoon of the pepper and blend until smooth, scraping down the jar as necessary. With the motor running, slowly add the olive oil. Taste, ideally with your wine, and add more salt and/or pepper if you like. (You can prepare the dressing up to a week in advance, storing it covered in the refrigerator. Return it to room temperature and, if necessary, restir before serving.)

■ Use a vegetable peeler to cut the ounce of cheese into thick shaves (you should have about ⅓ cup). Set aside. (You can shave the cheese up to a day in advance, storing it covered in the refrigerator.)

■ Prepare the grill to high heat and lightly oil the grate. Sprinkle the steak with the remaining ¾ teaspoon of salt and remaining ¼ teaspoon of pepper. Grill to desired doneness, about 4 minutes per side for medium rare. Remove the steak from the grill and let it rest, loosely covered with foil, for 5 minutes.

■ Meanwhile, in a large bowl, combine the romaine, radicchio, arugula, and onion with about two-thirds of the dressing. Arrange the mixture on a platter or plates, dividing it evenly.

■ Cut the steak across the grain diagonally into thin slices. Arrange the steak and sun-dried tomatoes over the salads, dividing them evenly. Drizzle with the remaining dressing, sprinkle with the shaved cheese, and serve.

spinach and parmesan polenta with grilled vegetable ragout

Warm, creamy, and cheesy—a bowl of Italian-inspired comfort food, that's what this is. Earthy spinach, sharp Parmesan, toasted walnuts, and a bit of fire-roasted flavor combine to deliciously tie this stew to the wine. • **Serves 4 to 6**

  1 fennel bulb, stalks and feathery tops trimmed
  4 plum tomatoes, halved lengthwise and seeded
  2 crookneck squash or yellow zucchini, quartered lengthwise
  2 zucchini, quartered lengthwise
  6 tablespoons extra virgin olive oil, divided
3½ teaspoons coarse kosher salt, divided, or more to taste
1½ teaspoons freshly ground black pepper, divided, or more to taste
  4 cloves garlic, pressed through a garlic press or minced
  4 teaspoons fresh lemon juice, or more to taste
  4 to 4½ cups low-sodium beef or vegetable broth
1⅓ cups polenta (see below)
  8 cups loosely packed baby spinach leaves (about 4 ounces)
  1 cup shredded Parmesan cheese (2½ to 3 ounces), divided
  ¼ cup chopped walnuts, toasted (see note on page 18)

■ Keeping the root end intact, cut the fennel bulb into 8 wedges. In a large bowl, combine the fennel, tomatoes, squash, zucchini, 3 tablespoons of the olive oil, 2 teaspoons of the salt, and 1 teaspoon of the pepper.

■ Prepare the grill to medium-high heat. Grill the fennel, squash, and zucchini until softened and lightly charred, 4 to 5 minutes per side. Grill the tomatoes, skin side down, until softened and lightly charred, about 2 minutes. Set aside until cool enough to handle.

■ Cut the fennel, squash, and zucchini into ½-inch dice. In the bowl of a food processor, combine half of the chopped vegetables with the tomatoes, garlic, lemon juice, and remaining 3 tablespoons of olive oil and pulse to make a coarse puree. Transfer the mixture to a medium saucepan and add the remaining chopped vegetables. Set aside. (You can prepare the ragout up to a day in advance, storing it covered in the refrigerator.)

■ In a large saucepan or small stockpot over high heat, bring 4 cups of the broth to a boil. Gradually add the polenta, whisking constantly. Return to a boil, reduce to a simmer, cover, and cook, stirring frequently and adding more broth a few tablespoons at a time if the polenta is too thick, until the polenta is tender, about 10 minutes. Remove from the heat and add the spinach, ¾ cup of the cheese, the remaining 1½ teaspoons of salt, and remaining ½ teaspoon of pepper. Stir until the spinach is wilted and the cheese is melted.

■ While the polenta is cooking, place the saucepan of ragout over medium heat and bring to a boil. Reduce to a simmer and cook until heated through, about 5 minutes. Taste, ideally with your wine, and add more lemon juice, salt, and/or pepper if you like. Cover and set aside.

■ Arrange the polenta in shallow bowls, dividing it evenly. Top with the ragout, remaining 1/4 cup of cheese, and walnuts and serve hot.

NOTE Polenta is available at most major supermarkets, often in the same section as the cornmeal. Besides using it in this recipe, you can use it in Merlot-Braised Lamb Shanks with Gorgonzola Polenta (page 138) and as a side dish or bed for other braises, sauces, and stews. (For the recipes in this book, don't use already-cooked polenta which comes in a large sausage shape and is usually found in the prepared foods section.) Since polenta sets up and becomes firm after cooking, make it as close to serving time as possible.

FOOD + WINE TIP Walnuts have a natural affinity with Cabernet. That papery coating around the nuts is loaded with tannins, complementing the tannins in the wine.

grilled sausages, peppers, and onions with dijon sour cream

Quick, easy, and satisfyingly hearty, this dish is ideal for a weeknight. But it's also great for a backyard party—because you can prepare everything in advance, then simply finish the skewers on the grill when everyone's ready to eat. • **Serves 6**

1 cup sour cream
¼ cup Dijon mustard
2 small red onions (about 12 ounces)
24 mini bell peppers
8 cooked sun-dried tomato chicken sausages (two 12-ounce packages), cut into 3 pieces each
6 tablespoons extra virgin olive oil
1½ teaspoons coarse kosher salt
¾ teaspoon freshly ground black pepper
Special equipment: twelve 10- to 12-inch skewers, soaked in water for at least 10 minutes if they're wood or bamboo

▪ In a small bowl, combine the sour cream and mustard. Set aside. (You can prepare the Dijon sour cream up to 3 days in advance, storing it covered in the refrigerator.)

▪ Keeping the root end intact, cut each onion into 12 wedges. Thread each skewer with 2 onion wedges, 2 peppers, and 2 pieces of sausage. (You can prepare the skewers up to a day in advance, storing them covered in the refrigerator.)

▪ Prepare the grill to medium heat. Brush the skewers with the olive oil and sprinkle with the salt and pepper. Grill until the vegetables are crisp-tender and lightly charred and the sausage is heated through, 4 to 5 minutes per side.

▪ Serve the skewers hot, with the Dijon sour cream on the side or drizzled on top.

duck breasts with cabernet–blue cheese pan sauce

In both taste and texture, duck is more like red meat than chicken, which is why it can work so well with a big red like Cabernet. As for blue cheese, it's polarizing—some say Cab and blue cheese is a bad idea, while others say it's classic. Me, I love it—but why not decide for yourself?

Ideally, buy a hunk of blue cheese and crumble it up. It'll melt more easily into the sauce than precrumbled. • **Serves 6**

6 boneless, skin-on duck breasts (2½ to 3 pounds)
1½ teaspoons coarse kosher salt, or more to taste
1 teaspoon freshly ground black pepper, or more to taste
1½ cups Cabernet Sauvignon, or other dry red wine
¾ cup crumbled blue cheese (about 3 ounces), divided
1 tablespoon chopped fresh chives

■ Trim any silver skin from the meaty side of the duck breasts. If the tender is still attached, scrape the tendon out and pat the tender back in place. Trim the skin to no more than ¼ inch overhang. Use a sharp knife to score the skin in a crosshatch pattern, with the cuts about ½ inch apart, being careful not to cut into the meat. Sprinkle both sides of the duck with the salt and pepper.

■ Heat two large skillets over medium-high heat. Add the duck, skin side down, and cook until medium brown, about 6 minutes. As the fat renders, spoon it off once or twice. Reduce the heat to medium and continue cooking until the skin is crisp and deeply golden brown, 2 to 4 minutes. Turn and cook until an internal thermometer reads 140°F for medium rare, 4 to 6 minutes. Transfer the duck to a cutting board and let it rest, loosely covered with foil, for 5 minutes.

■ Meanwhile, pour off the duck fat and return one of the skillets to medium-high heat (remove the other from the heat). Add the wine, scrape up any browned bits on the bottom of the skillet, and cook until reduced to ½ cup, about 8 minutes. Remove from the heat, add ½ cup of the cheese, and stir until it's melted. Taste the sauce, ideally with your wine, and add salt and/or pepper if you like.

■ Cut the duck on a diagonal into ½-inch slices. Arrange on a platter or plates and drizzle with the pan sauce. Sprinkle with the remaining ¼ cup of cheese and the chives and serve hot.

FOOD + WINE TIP Blue cheeses can vary in saltiness. If you find that your wine is tasting too sharp, your cheese might be on the mild side—just sprinkle on a little extra salt at the table.

lemon- and olive-stuffed leg of lamb

While the "stuffing" in this incredible roast is merely an easy-to-make tapenade, it infuses bright, complex flavors into the meat.

On the side, try sautéed spinach, braised greens, or rice with pine nuts. • **Serves 6 to 8**

1 lemon
½ cup drained pitted kalamata olives, plus more for garnish
2 tablespoons extra virgin olive oil
4 cloves garlic
1 tablespoon fresh thyme leaves
1 tablespoon fresh oregano leaves
2½ teaspoons coarse kosher salt, divided
1½ teaspoons freshly ground black pepper, divided
1 boneless leg of lamb (4½ to 5 pounds), excess fat trimmed

■ Cut the lemon in half lengthwise. Cut one half into slices and set aside. Cut the remaining half into 4 chunks.

■ In the bowl of a food processor, combine the lemon chunks (peel and all), olives, olive oil, garlic, thyme, oregano, ½ teaspoon of the salt, and ½ teaspoon of the pepper and pulse to make a chunky sauce, scraping down the bowl as necessary. Set aside.

■ Unroll the lamb and trim any silver skin from the inside of the leg. Spread the inside evenly with the olive mixture. Roll the leg up into a log shape and tie with kitchen twine at 1- to 1½-inch intervals. Sprinkle on all sides with the remaining 2 teaspoons of salt and remaining 1 teaspoon of pepper. Cover and refrigerate for 8 to 24 hours (see note on page 139).

■ Return the lamb to room temperature.

■ Preheat the oven to 450°F.

■ Arrange the lamb, fat side up, on a rack in a roasting pan large enough to comfortably hold it. Roast for 15 minutes.

■ Reduce the oven to 325°F and continue roasting until an internal thermometer inserted into the center of the meat reads 130°F for medium rare, 1¼ to 1½ hours total cooking time. Transfer the lamb to a cutting board and let it rest, loosely covered with foil, for 15 minutes. (It will continue to cook, reaching an internal temperature of about 140°F.)

■ Remove the twine and slice the lamb crosswise. Drizzle with the pan drippings, garnish with the olives and reserved lemon slices, and serve hot.

good old-fashioned pot roast

My mom used to make pot roast, sometimes on a weekend after-noon when we were hanging around the house doing jigsaw puzzles or watching ABC's *Wide World of Sports*, Mom's favorite show. The smells coming from the kitchen for hours—and hours!—were sort of a delicious tease, promising a meal worth waiting for. • **Serves 4 to 6**

   2 tablespoons all-purpose flour
   1 tablespoon coarse kosher salt, or more to taste
 1½ teaspoons freshly ground black pepper, or more to taste
     One 3½- to 4-pound boneless beef chuck roast, excess fat trimmed
   2 tablespoons extra virgin olive oil
   1 cup Cabernet Sauvignon, or other dry red wine
   1 cup reduced-sodium beef broth
   1 tablespoon balsamic vinegar, or more to taste
 1½ teaspoons soy sauce
   2 bay leaves
   4 sprigs fresh thyme
   4 carrots (about 1 pound), cut on the diagonal into 2- to 2½-inch pieces
   2 onions (about 1 pound)
   4 red potatoes (about 1 pound), quartered

▨ In a small bowl, combine the flour, salt, and pepper. Place the meat on a flexible cutting board or sheet of parchment and sprinkle on all sides with the flour mixture.

▨ In a skillet, braising pan, or Dutch oven large enough to comfortably hold the meat, over medium-high heat, warm the olive oil. Add the meat, shaking any excess flour onto the cutting board, and cook until well browned on all sides, 10 to 12 minutes (while the meat cooks, reserve any flour mixture that didn't adhere, using the cutting board to return it to the small bowl). Transfer the meat to a platter or plate. Set aside.

▨ Return the skillet to medium-high heat, add the wine, and scrape up any browned bits on the bottom. Cook until reduced by half, about 3 minutes. Stir in the broth, vinegar, soy sauce, bay leaves, thyme, and any reserved flour mixture, stirring to dissolve the flour and salt. Add the meat back to the skillet. Bring to a boil, reduce to a simmer, and cover (if your lid won't fit over the meat or you don't have one, create one with foil). Cook for 2 hours, carefully turning the meat halfway through.

▨ Add the carrots, nestling them into the liquid around the meat, and cook for 15 minutes.

▨ Meanwhile, keeping the root end intact, cut the onions into 6 wedges each.

■ Add the onions and potatoes and cook until the meat and vegetables are very tender, 45 to 60 minutes (if all the vegetables aren't
in the liquid, move them around halfway through). Transfer the meat
to a cutting board and let it cool slightly.

■ Meanwhile, use a slotted spoon to transfer the vegetables to a
bowl, platter, or plates. If you like, skim the fat from the sauce in the
skillet. Taste the sauce, ideally with your wine, and add more vinegar,
salt, and/or pepper if you like.

■ Cut the meat into ½-inch slices. Arrange the slices on a platter or
plates and spoon some of the sauce on top. Serve the remaining
sauce at the table.

cabernet + merlot = a perfect pairing

You know all those famous red wines from Bordeaux? Those wines
that are considered some of the best in the world? Well, they're mostly
blends of Cabernet Sauvignon and Merlot—along with Cabernet
Franc, Malbec, and Petit Verdot, to varying degrees—with each wine
contributing to and improving the others.

peppered prime rib roast with crème fraîche–horseradish sauce

If you're looking for a grand entrée to serve with a grand bottle of Cabernet Sauvignon, look no further. This is the king of roasts (and you don't have to tell your guests how easy it was to prepare). On the side, serve Yorkshire pudding, natch. • **Serves 6 to 8**

½ cup crème fraîche
½ cup heavy whipping cream
¼ cup prepared horseradish, or more to taste
2 tablespoons chopped fresh chives, or more to taste
½ teaspoon white pepper, ideally freshly ground, plus more to taste
2 tablespoons black peppercorns, plus freshly ground black pepper to taste
1 tablespoon coarse kosher salt, plus more to taste
8 bay leaves
4 cloves garlic, pressed through a garlic press or minced, plus 2 cloves garlic, smashed
1 tablespoon Dijon mustard
1 tablespoon extra virgin olive oil
One 7- to 8-pound standing rib roast, excess fat trimmed
2 cups reduced-sodium beef broth
Optional special equipment: electric spice or coffee grinder

▧ In the bowl of an electric mixer fitted with a whisk attachment, beat the crème fraîche and whipping cream on high speed to stiff peaks. Fold in the horseradish, chives, and white pepper. Taste, ideally with your wine, and add more horseradish, chives and/or white pepper if you like. Set aside in the refrigerator. (You can prepare the crème fraîche–horseradish sauce up to 2 days in advance, storing it covered in the refrigerator.)

▧ In an electric spice or coffee grinder, combine the black peppercorns, salt, and bay leaves and pulse to make a coarse powder. (If you don't have an electric spice or coffee grinder, finely crush the bay leaves as best you can with a mortar and pestle or your fingers and combine them with the salt and 2 tablespoons of freshly ground black pepper.) Transfer the spice mixture to a small bowl and stir in the pressed garlic cloves, mustard, and olive oil, making a paste. Rub the paste all over the roast. Cover and refrigerate for 8 to 24 hours (see note on page 139).

▧ Return the roast to room temperature.

▧ Preheat the oven to 450°F.

▧ Arrange the roast, fat side up, on a rack in a roasting pan large enough to comfortably hold it. Roast for 20 minutes.

■ Reduce the oven to 350°F and continue roasting until an internal thermometer inserted into the center of the meat without touching bone reads 130°F for medium rare (try to avoid any pockets of fat when checking the temperature), 1¾ to 2 hours total cooking time. Transfer the roast to a platter and let it rest, loosely covered with foil, for 30 minutes. (It will continue to cook, reaching an internal temperature of about 140°F.)

■ Meanwhile, drain the fat from the roasting pan. Place the pan on the stovetop over medium-high heat, straddled over two burners if necessary, and add the broth and smashed garlic cloves. Bring to a boil, scraping up the browned bits in the bottom of the pan. Remove from the heat and transfer to a saucepan.

■ Transfer the roast to a cutting board. Add any accumulated juices to the saucepan. Place the saucepan over high heat and bring to a boil. Reduce to a simmer and cook for 10 minutes. Taste, ideally with your wine, and add salt and/or ground black pepper if you like.

■ Carve the roast and serve hot, with the jus and the crème fraîche–horseradish sauce on the side.

new york steaks with espresso pan sauce

The sauce on these steaks might remind you of coffee-flavored Nips hard candies—without being sweet, it has rich, creamy coffee flavor. Combined with a meaty steak, it's delightfully surprising, yet moanfully good.

Like the candies, there's even a little crunch, thanks to crushed whole coffee beans sprinkled on top. • **Serves 2**

  6 whole espresso coffee beans
     Two 8- to 10-ounce New York steaks, about 1 inch thick
  1 teaspoon coarse kosher salt
  ¾ teaspoon freshly ground black pepper
  1 tablespoon extra virgin olive oil
  ½ cup brewed very strong coffee
  2 tablespoons (¼ stick) unsalted butter, cut into 3 or 4 pieces
  1 teaspoon Dijon mustard
  1 tablespoon heavy whipping cream

▨ Use a mortar and pestle to lightly crush the coffee beans. (If you don't have a mortar and pestle, place them in a small bowl and lightly crush them with the end of a wooden spoon.) Set aside.

▨ Sprinkle both sides of the steaks with the salt and pepper.

▨ In a large skillet over medium-high heat, warm the olive oil. Add the steaks and cook to desired doneness, about 3½ minutes per side for medium rare. Transfer the steaks to a platter or plates and let them rest, loosely covered with foil, for 5 minutes.

▨ Meanwhile, return the skillet to medium heat. Stir in the brewed coffee, scraping up any browned bits in the bottom of the skillet, and cook until reduced to a thin layer in the skillet, about 3 minutes. Remove the skillet from the heat, add the butter and mustard, and stir until the butter is melted. Stir in the cream.

▨ Top the steaks with the pan sauce. Garnish with the crushed coffee beans and serve hot.

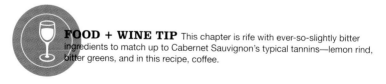

FOOD + WINE TIP This chapter is rife with ever-so-slightly bitter ingredients to match up to Cabernet Sauvignon's typical tannins—lemon rind, bitter greens, and in this recipe, coffee.

index

Note: Page references in *italics* refer to photographs.